Beyond the Chase

Beyond the Chase

Breaking Your Obsessions
That Sabotage True Intimacy

Carla Wills-Brandon

HAZELDEN®

Hazelden
Center City, Minnesota 55012
hazelden.org

ISBN: 978-1-59285-718-0

Library of Congress Cataloging-in-Publication Data
[add when available, and then delete the ISBN above the CIP]

Editor's note
The names, details, and circumstances may have been changed to protect the privacy of those mentioned in this publication.

This publication is not intended as a substitute for the advice of health care professionals.

Alcoholics Anonymous and AA are registered trademarks of Alcoholics Anonymous World Services, Inc.

13 12 11 10 09   1 2 3 4 5 6

Cover design by [name]
Interior design by Kinne Design
Typesetting by BookMobile Design and Publishing Services

To my own dance partner, Michael,
and to my "little dancers," Aaron and Joshua

i like you!

i do!

i really like you!

I think I love you!

I do!

I really LOVE you!

I MEAN it! I'm SERIOUS!

I NEED YOU!

I DO!

I MUST HAVE YOU!

RIGHT NOW!

I CAN'T LIVE WITHOUT YOU!

I'LL DIE!

what?

i've got you?

really?

umm...okay, what do we do now?

CONTENTS

FOREWORD

I was recently watching a popular television talk show devoted to the topic of sex. During one segment, the discussion centered on monogamy. The host was interviewing a very good-looking guy. Although the guest was dressed as if headed for an athletic day at the beach, he wasn't talking about nutritional supplements or protein powders. Instead, he'd made a name for himself promoting his own sexual cause. He believed men needed a variety of types of women for sexual purposes. I just had to call Carla out of the kitchen, where she was cooking up a new dish for supper.

As she walked into the study, we both heard the guest say, "Men want to have sex with all types of women all of the time. Cheating is normal! Women need to understand this, deal with it, and it's my job to convince them!" Carla burst out laughing. When asked by the interviewer about committed relationships and marriage, he replied, "Ridiculous! Fidelity isn't normal." Then he described how he'd made a fortune giving online suggestions to women who'd been cheated on, and I could tell Carla was now getting irritated. Shaking her head, she said, "Another parasite taking advantage of those who're emotionally in pain." With this, she went back to the comfort of preparing her Russian dish for that evening's meal.

After I set the dinnerware out, I turned back to the television set. Hearing the guest now angrily chastising helping professionals, I suspected he had some serious intimacy issues of his own. In spite of his high level of ignorance, our man did have one important thing to share. He insisted that cheating was based on biology.

Thousands upon thousands of years ago, for the human race to survive, it was necessary for one man to impregnate as many females as possible. Mortality rates were very high, and lust was essential for the continuation of the species. Without biological lust, none of us would be here. But even though promiscuity may have been key to the species' survival, we must remember that was a very long, long time ago. Today, the question we must ask ourselves is this: Will lust alone complete us?

Over the years Carla and I have counseled thousands of families and couples. Relationship difficulties are epidemic in today's society, and infidelity is just one of the many possible symptoms. Intimacy is an often misunderstood concept. Weekly, Carla and I work with couples and individuals who think they know what healthy intimacy is, but in actuality are clueless. These folks typically watch popular television talk shows and are often readers of the latest pop self-help books. Some of them are even longstanding members of self-help support groups. Though these very intelligent individuals may have a lot of information about intimacy, they still can't seem to create health within their own relationships. If you are one of those people, know first that you aren't alone, and second that help is here.

Michael Brandon

ACKNOWLEDGING ANGELS

Even after my agent and dear friend John White situated me with Hazelden, a dream publishing company, this book almost didn't happen. On September 13, 2008, Hurricane Ike sent a twenty-foot tide surge into Galveston Island, off the Texas coast, forcing me and my family to evacuate to nearby Houston. Once at the home of our cousins Ben and Joy Warren, we thought we were safe, but fate had different plans for us.

As the storm moved from Galveston to Houston, tornadoes began to touch down, dropping gigantic trees onto the roofs of nearby houses. I found myself hiding from Mother Nature's temper tantrum under a desk with my husband Michael, our youngest son Joshua, our golden retriever Fee Fee, and our cat Tom. It was a terrifying night, but thanks to Ben and Joy's safe haven, the following morning we emerged unhurt. Unfortunately, we were also without water, gas, and electricity in 95-degree heat. For the next three weeks we would live without these modern conveniences.

Wondering how on earth I'd complete this book without electricity to power my computer, I contacted Hazelden's editorial director, Sid Farrar. Sid told me not to worry, but to instead take care of myself and my family. He kindly let me know that Hazelden would be there to assist me when my life wasn't quite so chaotic. Hazelden's editorial coordinator, Kathy Anderson, had been waiting for my photograph for the book cover, along with other materials, but like Sid, she too was incredibly supportive and understanding. The staff at Hazelden responded with genuine care and kindness to my family's devastation. They have my deepest affection and appreciation.

After we'd been preparing meals by candlelight for nearly a week, my aunt Naomi Warren (known as Nuinui) let us know she had electricity. Along with some twenty other desperate family members, we descended upon her high-rise condominium at the Houstonian near downtown. For several weeks Nuinui provided us with a comfortable refuge where we could charge cell phones, wash clothes, cook meals, and spend a few hours basking in air conditioning. The staff at the Houstonian was more than understanding of our plight, and their generosity will forever be treasured.

When we finally had an Internet connection, I quickly composed an e-mail message to Hazelden. As I compiled some missing materials to send, I suddenly broke down in tears. Seeing my distress, Nuinui sat down with me, and soon she was sharing stories of survival from her time in Auschwitz, the Nazi death camp. Her courage and endurance during such a horrific time in history quickly put my life into perspective. Giving me a hug, she said, "You can do it!" With this I dried my eyes and finished the work I needed to do. Without my aunt's words of wisdom, I might have thrown in the towel that very day! Nuinui, I love you!

Returning to Galveston Island, my family was confronted with ten feet of water in our house and again, no electricity. It was surreal but reassuring to watch the American Red Cross travel down our debris-filled streets passing out food, ice, and water. Their dedication and charity were a godsend. Eventually, the electric companies rolled onto the island with massive equipment. Working sixteen hours a day, they got the lines up and running. Thank you, guys and gals! With electricity this book was finally completed.

The editor who then polished the manuscript for this book proved to be another gem. Karen Chernyaev is an author's delight. Not only did she smooth out the rough edges of the manuscript, she provided a great deal of support during my occasional computer crashes when I'd have my own post-Ike meltdown. The easy flow of words contained within these pages never would have happened without her talent and wealth of experience. Thank you, new friend!

Also responsible for the success of this book are my buddy Dick Slaughter, who received daily frantic telephone calls from me for weeks,

Bill and Willy King, who graciously agreed to wade through the wreckage of the hurricane and photograph me for this book, and all those who like myself had suffered the hammer of Ike. Without my wonderful friends, I wouldn't have found the strength to get through this trauma. Staying connected with my community helped me endure many emotional ups and downs. Sharing pain lessens the burden.

Finally, three months after the storm, my family and I still don't have heat in our home, but we do have each other. My sanity would be long gone if it weren't for my husband, Michael. When overwhelmed with the strain of the hurricane aftermath, he has given me the encouragement I've needed to stay focused on this project. My two sons have also proved what strong young men they are by stepping in without being asked and doing what needs to be done. I'm so very proud of both of them. To Michael, Aaron, and Joshua, I must say I know that these last few months I haven't been the most patient, calm, or rational wife or mother, and I apologize. In spite of this, know you are all more precious to me than life itself, and I love you.

Carla Wills-Brandon
December 25, 2008
Galveston Island, Texas

Asking Why When Love Goes Wrong Again

Lesson 1: Female Point of View

I'd marry again if I found a man who had 15 million and would sign over half of it to me before the marriage and guarantee he'd be dead within a year.

— BETTE DAVIS, HOLLYWOOD LEGEND

Lesson 2: Male Point of View

Ah, yes, divorce, from the Latin word meaning to rip out a man's genitals through his wallet.

— ROBIN WILLIAMS, ACTOR AND COMEDIAN

When our relationships fall apart, our first thought is, *What on earth went wrong? Everything seemed so perfect.* Distressed, we search for answers to explain the relationship failure but end up feeling even more confused. We suffer disappointment, loss, and intense loneliness. One temporary remedy for this sense of unbearable emptiness, we may find, is to try to block the pain with obsessive and addictive behaviors we've carried over from our past. We may turn to our old standbys—alcohol, drugs, gambling, overeating, overspending, even obsessing over our children or our religion. Or we may seek that one more relationship, the one that will give us that wonderful, can't-live-without-you feeling for life. But regardless of what we do, we end up with the same empty feeling.

The normal ebb and flow of a committed relationship means that we're bound to experience some lows. Empty feelings in a relationship are normal, but they're also temporary. How a relationship first gets to that low point is one thing, and we'll discuss that in depth in chapter 1. But how we respond to those low points is another. If we use addictive behaviors to cope with empty feelings in a relationship, we create barriers. Temporary lows become permanent struggles that prevent us from graduating to a healthy relationship, to a level of intimacy that can really make us feel content.

At the end of the day, no matter who we are drawn to or why, most of us long to be in a healthy, intimate relationship with a partner. But what does it mean to be intimate? Intimacy has many definitions. Knowing what a healthy, intimate relationship looks like for us is only half the battle. Once we know what we're really after, how do we get there and stay there? The issues that can interfere with a healthy relationship are endless, as are the means we use to avoid dealing with them. The trick is discovering what our own issues are and learning how to move beyond them.

True intimacy flourishes when we allow ourselves to be vulnerable with another human being. As we work through intimacy barriers, our vulnerability opens the door to an emotional connection with our partner on a deeper, more soul-touching level. In sharing who we really are with the person we most want to connect with, we begin to tear down the walls that separate us from one another. With such connectedness comes a feeling of acceptance, respect, friendship, support, admiration, safety, and trust. Intimacy also enables us to develop healthy physical, emotional, sexual, and even spiritual boundaries. With solid boundaries in place, we don't have to run from our relationship or chase the feeling we had when our relationship was exciting and new. And we don't have to resort to unhealthy behaviors when we hit those periodic stumbling blocks.

The following pages will guide you through the steps needed to identify, understand, and resolve the sources of your own intimacy blocks. You will also learn how to develop the skills needed to be intimate with a partner—and once that happens, the desire to continually reexperience the thrill of the chase will be replaced with a loving union with a partner, which is much more rewarding and meaningful. Come with me and find out just how well a relationship can work, and discover the true meaning of healthy intimacy for yourself.

• • •

1

The Thrill of the Chase

I detest "love lyrics." I think one of the causes of bad mental health in the United States is that people have been raised on "love lyrics."

— FRANK ZAPPA, COMPOSER, MUSICIAN, AND FILM DIRECTOR

The sultry legendary movie star Joan Crawford was right when she said that being in love can make you feel like a million dollars or send you straight into the depths of an emotional hell.

That truth has come home to me all too clearly in my work counseling couples—a practice I share with my husband, Michael. Over the last twenty-five years, we have worked with thousands of people who have had serious relationship problems. They never seek us out while in the throes of passion. Of course they don't—life feels wondrous when they're floating in a lust-filled, emotionally delicious new love affair. But for many people, relationships can seem to sour: sometimes quickly, sometimes slowly. Our offices are the last resort for people struggling to understand what went wrong. They can even be a refuge where the lovesick come to lick their wounds after a relationship dies a tragic death. The agony of painful love is often written on their faces; we can see it before they even open their mouths. We have helped clients recover from devastating romantic breakups, and we have also had the pleasure of watching couples heal into healthy relationships. All couples experience bumps in the road. The trick to surviving the bumps is knowing why they're there, how to push through them, and what to learn from them.

Many relationships end because couples are clueless when it comes to working through the difficulties. Clients typically make comments like these:

- *"Why didn't I see it coming? He just dumped me! Something wasn't feeling right about the relationship, and I suspected he was unhappy, but this? I don't get it! He never told me he thought there were problems, and I never asked! I can't believe he ended up being just like all the rest of them!"*

- *"How could I be so stupid? Why couldn't I see what she was really like? She was a train wreck, and her childhood stuff destroyed our relationship. Her relationship with her family made me nuts! She dumped her anger at her last husband on me, and I didn't deserve that. And when she wasn't mad at him, she was angry with me!"*

- *"Am I blind? Why do I continue to put up with this garbage? Why can't I put my foot down and say, 'No more!' He drinks like a fish and spends too much time with his buddies. He never seems to have time for me. It's always beer and the boys."*

- *"She had an affair—again. This time it was my best friend. Last time I forgave her, but this time I don't know what I'll do."*

- *"When we were first dating, he was so sweet and kind. That man swept me off my feet and made me feel like a princess. Two years later, you'd think I was an albatross around his neck. He never even looks at me. He makes me feel stupid, unattractive, fat, and unlovable. He's never home, he forgets my birthday, and sex is nonexistent. What happened?"*

The Perfect Mate?

Every one of us has a few warts, quirks, defects of character, hidden peculiarities, or baggage. None of us is perfect. Imperfection is part of the human condition, and most flaws are entirely normal. When we start a new relationship, however, our infatuation paints our mate as a picture of perfection. Our blinded mind's eye portrays the new partner as the "right one" before we even get to know each other. Over time, this aura fades and our mate's imperfections are exposed, yet many of us fight to keep the blindfold on. And if it slips, we tell ourselves the warts aren't all that bad.

In healthy relationships, imperfections eventually come to light and we either address them or accept them. But problem relationships, those doomed to fail, play out differently. Here, an imperfection becomes an excuse to abandon a relationship. A character defect such as raging behavior is used as a method of control. "It's not my fault! I can't help it!" we—or our partner—might say. "I just lose control of my anger when you don't answer the phone!" Before we know it, the relationship has ended and again we find ourselves wondering, *What went wrong? This feels just like my last relationship!*

How is it that so many of us can't see potential problems from the beginning? When we do finally get wind of them, why are they such a surprise? If we know that imperfection is a part of the relationship experience, why does such common sense elude us when we need it most? And even if we don't notice a partner's everyday quirks and harmless flaws at first, how is it that the obvious, telltale, neon-blazing signs of trouble also go right over our heads? Why are so many of us blinded by simple magnetism? The answer may lie with Mother Nature.

Mother Nature Strikes—Again and Again and Again

It's late in the afternoon and I'm beat. The sun is sinking and the sticky Gulf breeze is stirring. After a long, exhausting day, I'm almost ready to make my way home from the office where I counsel clients. After brewing a cup of herbal tea, I close the door to my office and turn to face my last client of the day: I'll call her Diane.

She is all aglow, exuberant with life, absolutely on fire. The middle-aged woman sitting on my couch is a very attractive and successful professional, the single mother of two teenage boys. Dark, short curly hair frames her porcelain face, and one would never guess she is over fifty. Dressed for the office in a pink silk pantsuit, she has already removed her fashionable fuchsia pumps and made herself quite at home.

Last week Diane had been dressed in black from head to toe, inside and out. Depression seeped from her every pore and saturated the room. I could feel the heaviness of her despair. A broken romance was at the core of it. For months she had been trying to make the relationship work, and then suddenly it just crumbled. He walked out and she didn't understand why.

This week, not only had her color scheme brightened, her frame of mind had as well. But knowing her as I did, my immediate thought was, *Oh, no. What's his name?* After taking a sip of tea I asked, "So who is the new man in your life?" Smiling back at me, she replied, "You know me that well?" Diane and I had been here before.

Her first marriage was to a man who seemed to lose interest in her as the years passed. At the end of a typical day, after they had spent eight hours immersed in their jobs, she would ask her husband, "Honey, how was your day?" Being a man of few words, he would typically answer, "Fine," or "When's dinner?" but he never seemed interested in her day. They spent their evenings behind the buffering screens of newspapers or computers, or with dinner trays in front of the television.

As hard as she tried, Diane couldn't seem to find the key to unlock the steel door he had closed on their relationship just months after their marriage. After they had children, the marriage became even more distant. Eventually, the pain and loneliness became overwhelming.

Finally, after completing college courses and finding a higher-paying job, Diane threw in the towel, packed up her two small children and walked out of the emotionally isolating prison of a marriage she had been locked into for almost a decade. Since that time, she had been involved with several lovers, but there had been problems with these relationships as well.

Diane showed up on my doorstep when she began to realize that her relationships were not only beginning similarly, they were ending similarly too. Last week, one more love affair had died a tragic death. Her emotions had ranged from blue emptiness to tearful grief to vengeful rage. But now, a week later, all the intense emotion surrounding that relationship had suddenly evaporated into thin air. Today we were at another "new beginning."

"He is just the cutest thing," Diane sighed. "The man is absolutely darling, has an incredible job, and emotionally seems really healthy." In the first thirty minutes of the session, she didn't refer to her most recent breakup even once. Instead, she was off to the races, already plotting out life with a new love interest. "I can see myself marrying this one," she announced. Seeing the skepticism on my face, she quickly added, "No, seriously. I know I said that about the last guy, but this time it's for real."

Picking up my teacup, I asked, "How long have you known him?" Tucking her legs under herself, Diane replied, "About a week, but it seems like I've known him forever. We really connected." Watching her, I could tell her mind was made up. She was lost in the illusion of his perfection. I would need to pull back and let her play this one out. As she continued to talk, I watched biology take over.

As she described her latest man's looks, her cheeks flushed and her eyes glowed, and as she named all his wonderful qualities, she became even more animated and excited. It was as if someone had just slipped her a sugar-coated happy pill. So intense was her happiness, for a few moments I thought she would actually levitate right off the couch.

Diane ended by saying, "I think I'm in love." Sipping tea, I thought to myself, "Physiology has taken over and drugged her again."

Mother Nature Takes Control

When a man or woman first meets a new love interest, the feeling is often intoxicating. Life is suddenly a joy twenty-four hours a day—a heaven on earth. Our priorities change and we focus all our attention on the source of this intoxication. We often think of it as love at first sight, divine fate, or the discovery of a true soul mate. But is it love or lust?

Let's put it this way: love involves an emotional experience—we feel a gentle fondness, affection, respect, and appreciation for another person. But lust is more about science. When physical attraction takes hold, physiological changes occur—highly mood-altering shifts in chemistry. Let's take a closer look at the chemical transformation associated with initial attraction, or, in other words, Mother Nature in action.

The Powerful Love Drug

Is it love? Is it lust? Or is it phenylethylamine? The thought of this hormone, referred to as PEA, doesn't exactly spark romantic visions of passionate love. Though it sounds more like some terrible disease, believe it or not, PEA is the substance at the base of lustful attraction. Which leads us to wonder: what is the difference between true love and hormonally driven lust? I'm often asked this question by people who are having difficulty developing meaningful long-term relationships. To give an adequate answer, I found it necessary to brush up on my chemistry.

What are the physical symptoms of love? "Sweaty palms, shaky knees, general restlessness, loss of appetite and the butterflies in the stomach syndrome" are caused by a natural brain chemical, phenylethylamine, commonly dubbed the "love molecule," notes Helen Fisher in her book *Why We Love*. Its release can be triggered by such deceptively simple actions as meeting another's eyes or touching hands. Heady emotions, racing pulses, and heavy breathing result. All of these symptoms can (unfortunately) be clinically explained as an overdose of phenylethylamine. In Fisher's words, "Phenylethylamine (which speeds up the flow of information between cells), dopamine (which makes us glow and feel good), and norepinephrine (which stimulates the production of adrenalin), make our world go round, our eyes sparkle and our heart beat faster."

So is the intense high we feel at the beginning of a new relationship the result of an overdose of love, or merely lust? Can this hormone wreak havoc on common-sense thinking and blind us to the obvious? Returning to the fiftysomething professional woman sitting on my office couch, talking about her latest boyfriend like a lovesick schoolgirl, we see that chemistry has taken over. Diane's breath quickens as she describes the brilliant blue of his eyes, the shades of salt and pepper in his hair, and the smoothness of his hands. As she gently rubs her own palms together, I notice sweat is being released through her pores and her mood is heady, as if she had taken a long sip of wine. She is experiencing an overdose of phenylethylamine.

His touch sent a spark through her body that went not to her heart but straight to her brain. His physical being triggered her biological bells and chemical fireworks. With each encounter with this new lover, more PEA will build up in Diane's system, making the attraction and magnetism even more powerful. No, Cupid didn't pierce her heart with arrows dipped in a love potion. Instead, her own brain flooded her with mood-altering chemicals as powerful as any illegal narcotic.

"The euphoria of falling in love is a kissing cousin (so to speak) of the euphoria you feel when you're doped to the gills for a root canal," says Edward Willett, a columnist summarizing the topic for readers of the Regina (Saskatchewan) *Leader-Post* on [add date]. "Many of the chemicals our bodies release when we come in contact with someone we find attractive are similar to amphetamines. One of them [PEA] . . . literally makes you high and causes you to do silly things like break into song in a crowded elevator."

But as the body's tolerance to PEA gradually rises, the euphoria fades—over several years, if not faster. Meanwhile, some people crave that initial high so acutely that they pursue other relationships in search of it. But if we stay with one person for the long term, we may find that our brain chemistry eventually works in our favor: our endorphin levels rise naturally if we are exposed continually to one particular person in a stable, positive way. These soothing, natural "feel-good" brain chemicals confer a sense of safety and peace. The down side is that when that relationship ends—through death or otherwise—the pain can feel as intense as an addict's withdrawal symptoms, since in fact, the chemistry is similar.

"Most scientists are now willing to concede that the capacity and desire to love is hardwired into our genetic makeup," notes Willett. He recounts one evolutionary explanation: About four million years ago our ancestors started standing upright, thereby displaying their physical and sexual characteristics more clearly—to potential mates among others. Suddenly, the process of choosing a mate became more complex, more personal, we might say. The potential for romance was born. And, he adds, "The pair-bonding that romance engenders, in turn, had an evolutionary benefit in that it increased the likelihood the offspring of the mating would survive."

Why Mother Nature Does That Thing She Does

During adolescence and young adulthood, we are physically at our best, like ripe plums ready for plucking. The skin is smooth, the body strong, the hair shiny, and youthful beauty saturates us. There is a reason for this abundance. As far as Mother Nature is concerned, this is baby-making time! At this point in life, biology is gearing us up to propagate the species. It's that simple. Phenylethylamine is necessary for the continuation of humankind. Lots of PEA flowing through the body eventually leads to lots of sex. Mother Nature is hoping lots of sex will produce lots of babies!

But once PEA has done its job and we have met our mate, the intense feelings of infatuation or lust eventually level off and then die down. After two or three years with the same partner, the initial euphoria fades or even takes a nosedive. Why? Some researchers believe that the body develops a type of resistance to our partner's own PEA. Constant exposure to the same hormone coming from the same person builds in us a tolerance to that individual's particular chemical makeup.

"Love Drug" Withdrawal

We know that over time, alcoholics develop a tolerance to alcohol: they need more booze to get the same buzz they originally felt with less. It appears that this same process of tolerance building takes place with the lust hormones. To get the same mind-altering rush experienced at the beginning of the relationship, we must seek new sources of it, along with new triggers.

If we don't, the lower levels of PEA in the brain may feel like a painful drug withdrawal at first. By now the blinders are off and the imperfections in the relationship are exposed. The painkilling anesthesia of this hormone has temporarily covered up our lows, our disappointments, hurts, griefs, and relationship problems. And once PEA production slows down, the unfinished business of life returns.

Because of the addictive qualities of PEA, many people are actually addicted to the chase—not for the pursuit for true love, but simply for that initial high in a relationship, for phenylethylamine. Some people seek out this high and are constantly looking to relationships to regain it. They believe it is this feeling that constitutes true love. The thought is, "If that feeling isn't there, I must not love this person." These individuals truly need the touch of PEA in order to have a relationship. When that's gone, so is the relationship.

I am often asked by those in troubled partnerships, "What happened to that great feeling? Where did it go? What's wrong with the relationship? It doesn't feel the way it did in the beginning. What went wrong? Do I need to get out of it?" The answers are usually simple. The effects of PEA have worn off, and now the real work must begin. Those bumps in the road have appeared, and to keep the relationship alive, the issues must be accepted or addressed.

The Real Thing

Couples often think that diminishing lust means their love is on the skids. This is far from true. If a couple is willing to work together and to move through the newly discovered flaws that PEA had temporarily blinded them to, eventually a different type of physiological change will occur. If a couple can stick it out, another group of powerful hormones—endorphins—will replace the self-made high of PEA. Scientists believe this new influx of hormones has a more lasting quality. Tolerance doesn't build, and these particular good feelings can remain consistent over very long periods of time.

When my hubby walks into the room, my brain is triggered to release more endorphins, those natural feel-good chemicals. Unless he has tromped through the house with muddy shoes, left the toilet seat up, or thrown his clothes in the middle of the floor, I typically feel myself relax when I'm with him. Indeed, many people in long-term relationships talk about feeling secure, comfortable, and serene when with their partner. They may also talk about how sex changes. Lustful sex still happens, but there is a level of intimacy that makes it better than ever. The sex makes them feel connected, and couples often talk about the spiritual qualities of intimate lovemaking.

Couples I have worked with who have evolved to this stage of the relationship describe how the company of their partner actually has a comforting effect on them. And statistically, people who are in long-term relationships live longer than single folks.

So What's the Real Problem?

Here's part of the problem: too many men and women give up too soon! They pack up and leave a relationship before the real magic can happen, because they fail to recognize that life is full of ups and downs, they don't want to bother with those bumps, or they use addictive behaviors to deal with them. Hard times between couples are normal—in fact, they're necessary in order to start building intimacy, the next phase of a healthy relationship. The intimate experience of feeling truly connected emotionally, physically, and spiritually with another person can't take place as long as this intoxicating chemical is coursing through our veins. Intimacy building begins *after* PEA production decreases. Unfortunately, instead of staying in the relationship and working through the issues that surface—and they will surface—we may respond in our customary way. We drink, eat, spend, or look for another mind-altering hit of phenylethlamine.

Remember my client Diane? The week before she arrived with news of her latest love, she had been dressed in black, her skin pale, her mood extremely low. She was in despair about not only a broken relationship, but about numerous family problems. She had been cleaning up her last failed romance and investigating the early death of her father. Her mother was in the hospital, both her sons had left for college, and her ex-husband was refusing to foot his share of the bill for their education. The weight of life was resting on her shoulders.

Without a relationship, Diane had no phenylethylamine to fix her feelings. It was time for her to do some work on herself. During that session, Diane began to dig deeper. She was finally feeling emotions she had been avoiding for years. Her work wasn't going to continue for long, though. By the following week she'd made a 180-degree turn. She'd met a man and felt the phenylethylamine again. But as in her previous relationship, the effects of the hormone pumping through her body began to fade and once again she was faced with her reality.

Building Intimacy When Mother Nature Lets Go

Back at the office, it's a week later and close to the end of another long workday. I'm hoping the peppermint tea I've just brewed will wake me up. As I make my way to my last client of the day, I see it's raining outside and I dread the drive home. Taking my seat, I see Diane is in her usual spot, but this time she is hugging a pillow. Gone is the pink silk and the glow in her eyes. I can tell trouble has begun. She's back in black and I think to myself, *It ended already?* Yes, in fact. Her new Prince Charming turned out to be just like the others, leaving her feeling alone and aggrieved one more time.

To sustain a healthy relationship, true intimacy building must be set in motion. Like many women and men in society today, this pretty client of mine not only feared true intimacy, she was attracted to men who were obsessed with the chase and addicted to the initial mood-altering feelings associated with phenylethylamine. When it was time for her to really look at her lovers' imperfections and confront their intimacy challenges, her relationships fell to pieces time and time again.

What did I suggest she do? First, I suggested she declare a thirty-day "no contact" period with this most recent past lover. In clinical circles this is also known as a phenylethylamine detoxification period. To help Diane return to her own life, to refocus on her unfinished business, and to begin healing from past losses and failed relationships, her own body had to be detoxified from the lust and romance chemicals it had produced. This could only happen if she abstained from contacting this past lover, painful as that might be. Along with this, our lady in black had to agree not to participate in another relationship for at least three months.

Diane followed through on these suggestions and cleaned up a great deal of her emotional baggage. Then she was in a position to experience a healthy relationship. Today, she has been in a committed, loving relationship for several years.

Are You Ready for the Real Thing Called Love?

Understanding the power of phenylethylamine is the first step toward building healthy relationships. Half the battle is simply knowing that this hormone temporarily prevents us from accurately seeing the person we're attracted to. Once the veil of intoxication is lifted, we are confronted with real intimacy challenges. At this point, we need to ask ourselves these questions:

- Can I accept or address the problem areas involved in this relationship?

- Will my partner try to work with me in this relationship to move through these difficulties?

- Are both of us committed to growing together?

Understanding that challenges will arise is essential. If you can answer yes to just one of the above questions, you are ready to begin addressing these challenges. All relationships have stumbling blocks. If we don't have the tools to chip away at these difficulties, we can find ourselves neck-deep in resentment, disappointment, confusion, and frustration. Most problems couples face can be resolved. It takes a bit of hard work, but the journey is worth it. If you are single and find yourself in one miserable relationship after another, know this: help is here. By doing the necessary work and committing to a path of healing, you will find yourself on the road to a meaningful and fulfilling long-term relationship.

We've now seen how the romantic chase can create a chemical high that can become addictive and block real intimacy. In this book we'll unmask some other common obsessive and addictive behaviors that we use to alter our brain chemistry and sabotage intimacy. But first, in the next two chapters, we'll see how the thought patterns and beliefs that cause these behaviors may have deep roots in our past.

· · ·

2

The Acorn Doesn't Fall Far from the Tree: How We Learn about Relationships

A guy is a lump, like a doughnut. So first you gotta get rid of all the stuff his mom did to him. And then you gotta get rid of all that macho crap they pick up from beer commercials.

— ROSEANNE BARR, COMEDIAN, ACTRESS, AND WRITER

The woman sitting on the old leather couch was beside herself with uneasiness, and she couldn't sit still. It was obvious to me that June hadn't slept in several nights and that she wasn't eating properly. Dark circles shadowed her eyes. Her brown pixie-cut hair was standing on end and she hadn't bothered with make-up.

"I just can't take it anymore, and I feel like I'm going to scream. Geez, I wish I could scream!" she cried as she pounded her fist into the soft pillow at her side. It was a chilly, early spring day and I had turned up the heat in the office hours ago. In spite of this, June had taken my grandmother's handmade blue afghan sitting on the couch and wrapped herself in it from head to toe. "Why can't Richard see I'm stressed out to the max?" she cried.

As the tears started to fall, I handed her a big box of tissues. It wasn't time for me to say a thing yet. At that moment, my job was just to listen. As June dabbed her tears, she sighed and said, "My father died a month ago. My oldest son went off to college three months ago, I feel like my life is falling apart, and Richard still expects me to be the hostess with

17

the mostest for his damn business dinners! Doesn't he realize I feel like I'm losing my mind?" She pulled the afghan more tightly around her thin frame. "And, as you know, I've been trying to wean myself off these horrible pain medications. Who would have believed a hysterectomy would lead to drug addiction? Hell, I thought for sure I was going to have to go back into the hospital to detoxify off all of these medicines." More tears trickled down her face. I could see she was feeling lost and alone in her pain and grief.

Looking at me with despair, June asked, "Can't you make him understand I'm on overload? During our next couples session, can't you explain it to him, or maybe Dr. Michael can talk to him? Richard just doesn't seem to get it! He really believes I should be over my grief about my dad's sudden death. And as if that weren't enough, he thinks I should be totally recovered from my hysterectomy, happy our son has left home, and emotionally 'fixed' now that I'm detoxing off these stupid pills!" Picking up the pillow next to her, she hugged it tightly and began rocking back and forth as she broke down and sobbed.

After several minutes of hard crying, June blew her red nose and pulled a bottle of water out of her oversized handbag. After taking a swig, she loosened the afghan and sat Indian style on the couch. The cry had done her good and she was calmer. Tucking her feet under the blanket, she said, "Wow! I didn't know *that* was going to happen. It all came up so suddenly. I haven't cried like that in ages!" She took a long drink of water. "You know, I can't cry around Richard. He absolutely hates it when I cry. But lately I feel like I'm choking back the tears more and more, and I just can't handle it much longer. I'm tired of making sure I'm in check so that everyone else around me is okay. It's doing me in!" Sighing again, she took another sip from her water bottle.

Seeing that June was now in a position to listen, I said, "You have a ton of grief. Not only has your father passed away, but your son has moved on. He is no longer a little boy, but a young man with feelings, ideas, and opinions of his own. Yes, your son is happy, away at college and doing well, but his moving out of your home changes your relationship with him, and that too is a huge loss." As I said this, the tears began to well up in her eyes again.

Regardless of this, I continued, "I know we've talked about how difficult your relationship with you father was, but that doesn't mean his death isn't going to be extremely upsetting. Yes, he was a very verbally abusive alcoholic, but you do have good memories too. Along with this, having a hysterectomy is just one more enormous grief issue. Anytime we have a major illness or surgery, we experience a strong sense of loss. Your surgery was female-related and though it was necessary, now you can't have any more babies. For you this is a big loss because I know you wanted more children. Weaning yourself off drugs that not only blunted your physical pain but buffered you from your emotions—that's like taking an ice cube out of the freezer and placing it in the hot summer sun. As you detox, you are also emotionally defrosting and you can no longer push those feelings away."

June looked at me with a pained expression. "Why do you get it, and I only see you once every two weeks, while Richard, who I am with day in and day out, is oblivious? He's seems to believe everything is just fine! And he makes me feel guilty if I even suggest there are major problems going on. I swear, he's just like his mother. She is totally unaware of others, their needs, wants, and desires. It's always about her, her health, her problems, and how no one appreciates her! When she heard I was getting a hysterectomy, she told me to quit sniveling, that lots of women had the surgery. And Richard is just like her. He probably has no idea I'm in this much pain, because he refuses to hear about it and won't see it!"

Watching her move from grief to anger, I replied, "Yes, most likely he is clueless. He learned how to feel feelings and have emotion by watching his parents experience or not experience their own emotions. Have you ever considered that your expectations of him may be unrealistic? Chances are he doesn't even know where to begin when it comes to feeling strong emotion. Who would have modeled this for him? If he doesn't know how to have his own feelings, how on earth is he ever going to be able to recognize your distress?"

June looked surprised, as if this were new information for her to consider. After a few seconds I decided to continue. "It would be nice if Richard were able to support you when you needed to cry. It would be lovely if he could take you in his arms and hold you when you were sad, but maybe he doesn't even know when you are depressed or upset. Detoxing from the medications is just the start of your healing from addiction, and it would be great if he recognized just how difficult this was for you. If Richard was aware of your grief, maybe he wouldn't keep pressuring you to do these dinner parties for his business clients, but what are you going to do if this doesn't change? What are you going to do if he continues to not react to your pain as you expect him to? What will you do to take care of yourself?"

Running her fingers through her hair in exasperation, June replied, "I don't think he *will* change, and I can't stand it. I love him, and I don't want to divorce him, but right now I can't stand being around him. He is so needy and demanding of my attention. And I can't ever be in a bad or sad mood! It's exhausting! I wish I could just get away for a while. I can't take care of him and be this exploding mess of emotion all at once."

Because June was feeling so trapped, she didn't even recognize she had come up with a solution to her dilemma. "Where would you go if you wanted to take a break from Richard and focus more on your own healing?" I asked. Surprised, June replied, "Well, I'd never really do this, but my parents bought a townhouse some years back. It's fully furnished, and no one is living in it right now. I guess I could go there, but I'd never do that, just move out and leave. It would hurt Richard if I left like that."

Challenging her, I pointed out, "But you just told me living with him is suffocating you, that he won't let you cry, and that you want to scream. You said he is needy but unable to be there for you. And in spite of all of the overloading emotion and grief you are feeling, he still expects you to put on these major dinner parties for him and his clients. Those concerns sound like good reasons to take a break, continue detoxing, get some space, rest, and allow yourself to heal, away from Richard and the stress of the relationship."

Looking very uncomfortable and defensive, June threw off the afghan and said, "No, it wouldn't work. Besides, what would my son think? And my mother? Oh my God, my mother would be mortified. My mother stood by my father even when his drinking was at its worst. No, I just can't do that." A few moments of uneasy silence passed. Then I said, "Well, you just told me that Richard was a lot like his mother. I heard you blame him for not seeing your stress and doing something about it to help you. But it seems to me that you too are a great deal like your own mother, and I also heard resistance to changing this."

I went on, "Your mother did not take care of herself in her relationship with your father. In the past we have talked about how emotionally abusive your father was when he drank and how you witnessed him calling her terrible, degrading names. Staying and putting up with that was not in your mother's best interest, nor did it do your father any good. Most of all, it was detrimental to you. What your mother did was enable your father to never take responsibility for his drinking or his behavior."

June looked shocked. I could tell she didn't like what I was saying, but I wasn't going to stop. "By staying and enduring abuse when your father was drunk and on a verbal tirade, your mother kept him from getting in touch with how his behavior was hurting not only her, but you. In other words, your mother was a big part of the problem. She actually allowed the behavior to continue by not taking care of her own needs. In not taking care of her needs, she didn't protect you."

With eyes wide open, June said, "You mean my mother did the wrong thing? But if she had left, who knows what my father would have done! He could have gotten into his car, driven drunk, and been pulled over by the police. I can't blame my mother. She did the best she could." I sat silently for a minute and then said, "I agree with you that most likely, at that time, your mother did the best she could under the circumstances, but that still doesn't change how it impacted you. Maybe if your father had been taken to jail for driving while intoxicated, and suffered consequences for his alcoholic behavior without your mother buffering for him, he might have begun to see that he had a serious problem with alcohol. If this had happened, maybe he would have gotten sober and become the father you always wanted."

June was obviously upset with this new revelation. Leaving my chair to sit next to her on the couch, I added, "You say that your husband is unaware of your needs and that he is incapable of recognizing you are on overload. This is happening because in his eyes, he sees you as doing well. You are enabling Richard to not see the marriage for what it is by continuing to not take care of yourself, your grief, and the losses you have recently experienced. Like your mother, you are buffering for him by not taking action that says, 'This is unacceptable behavior and it's not in my best interest.' Instead, you continue to wait for him to 'get' that you are having difficulty and that there are problems in the marriage. What would happen if you went to your parents' townhouse and took some time for yourself? Just packed a little bag and left? I suspect this physical action of desperation for self-care would indicate loudly to Richard that not all is well."

After taking another sip of her water, June sat quietly in thought for a few moments. Then she said, "My leaving would definitely get his attention. He couldn't ignore that, but what about my son? My boy has just started college and will be devastated if I leave his father. He has no idea things are as bad as they really are. I can't do this to him."

She still isn't getting it, I thought to myself. *She's looking for excuses to not be responsible for her own well-being.* Then I said, "You and Richard have modeled for your son some very dysfunctional relationship behaviors. Both of you are passing on to him the tragic relationship communication lessons you inherited from your own families. Chances are they learned these dysfunctional communication tactics from their own parents, your grandparents. Teaching our children that it's all right for couples to take time away from one another to sort out their differences is a healthy thing to do. Along with this, we need to model honest talk about relationship problems so that resolution can occur. You and Richard have extreme difficulty talking openly and honestly with one another. Both of you have modeled the famous "No Talk" rule to your son." Again, June looked surprised.

"You and Richard have never resolved your intimacy problems because he believes if problems are ignored they will just evaporate," I went on. "You enable him in this belief by not taking the action necessary to be responsible for your own feelings and healing. You won't honestly communicate with him. Instead you just bury your emotions. Then you wait for him to acknowledge that you are emotionally in a difficult spot, as opposed to doing what you need to take care of yourself. This is what your son has learned about relationships from you and his father. If you don't model something different, he will do the same in his relationships."

June was no longer defensive, but instead astounded. "Ouch! The 'No Talk' rule? I'm modeling this behavior for my son and I'm enabling Richard to avoid what's really going on in the marriage? Wow, that's quite a load of responsibility. I had no idea. So my taking a break and going to the townhouse would not only be good for me, but for Richard and my son too?"

Smiling, I thought to myself, *Finally we're getting somewhere!*

The Acorn Doesn't Fall Far from the Tree

My husband, Michael, and I have been married for thirty years. One could say we've established a successful foundation for a healthy relationship. I am a licensed marriage and family therapist with years of training and decades of clinical experience. Michael is a licensed clinical psychologist who's been in private practice since 1980. He studied with several world-renowned clinicians who specialize in the arena of relationships and relationship issues. Did our clinical background prepare us to create a healthy long-term relationship? Is that why we're still together?

Before we examine that question, let's look at our family histories. Michael comes from an interesting family. Both of his parents were well-educated Europeans who immigrated to the United States and became extremely successful. His father was a prominent surgeon while his mother was a well-respected university professor. Dinner at the Brandon house was always a unique cultural experience with great food and passionate conversation on the arts, literature, politics, and ancient history. Though I learned a great deal during my years at the Brandon dinner table, certain subjects were never brought up.

With their children present, Michael's parents could intellectually discuss and dissect the political happenings in the Middle East, but they rarely talked about the frightening difficulties their relatives in Israel were facing. As a matter of fact, if they did discuss family problems of any sort, they usually did so in four to five languages, all at once, so that the children wouldn't know what the parents were talking about. Michael's mother had lost her own mother to the gas chambers in Auschwitz, and his father's father had died suddenly from malaria in Europe. This was heavy history, but it was never discussed openly.

Michael's parents rarely talked about serious relationship concerns in front of him, and though their emotions could become heated over the latest art exhibit they'd seen together, he never saw them fight. Outside appearances suggested his intellectual parents were also happy and well-adjusted, but behind closed doors the tension between the two of them was often unbearable. As Michael put it, "I could hardly breathe! They didn't act angry, but you could sure feel the rage in the air. It was like walking across a thin layer of ice covering a deep, angry, rushing river."

In my family there were also secrets—lots of secrets—but we handled them differently. My father's side of the family had emigrated from Russia just before the Russian Revolution began between the late 1800s and early 1900s.Many of the relatives left behind in Russia were deported to gulags or concentration camps in northern Siberia during the cold war. None were ever heard from again. But no one in my father's family ever openly discussed this immense grief. As my grandfather said, "The past is the past. Leave it alone!" Unfortunately, the trauma of this history didn't go away. Instead, the emotions and loss were acted out very violently within the family, setting up generations of addiction, mental illness, and unhappiness.

On my mother's side, her only brother had been killed in Germany during World War II when he was just twenty years old. I knew almost nothing about this tragedy until I was an adult. No one ever openly grieved or asked questions about it. Though I saw the photographs of his coffin, it wasn't until years later that I learned my grandparents and mother never really knew if his body was actually lying inside.

Though these dark secrets were never discussed, they didn't just evaporate into thin air. Our families may have not talked about the old wounds and losses, but the unhealed anger, grief, depression, shame, and fear still existed. Instead, like old, worn-out suitcases containing moldy, dirty, disintegrating clothing, this heavy emotional baggage was passed down from one generation to the next. Opening them and letting a little cleansing fresh air in wasn't going to happen, so the unresolved feelings about these tragedies seeped out the seams. Disguised as current-day difficulties and attached to problems in the here and now, these emotions were then expressed in later generations as dysfunction.

Sadly, I don't think either of my parents realized how those secrets impacted their lives, and their life together. They fought openly, but didn't see that those generations of unexpressed emotion, teamed up with current-day stresses and feelings, were in fact deadly ammunition. They created an emotional atomic bomb! Because of the openness of their warring, all adult topics were laid out in plain sight for my sisters and me to see. Many of these issues were too hot for our childish minds to comprehend, but like our parents and their parents before them, we too absorbed rage, terror, and grief that were never ours to begin with.

So our families of origin may have inherited some similar tragedies, but they managed those facts very differently. Michael's family not only buried their trauma, they also tried to box up any related feelings. So, although their emotions were never completely contained, his parents looked functional. My family also hid the truth, but they externalized those emotions with extreme acting-out behavior. In other words, to the outside world they looked pretty nutty!

Now, considering the life experiences noted above, which of the following would you guess to be true of Michael and me?

a) Having seen our parents and grandparents' self-destructive ways of handling conflict, we subconsciously knew how to avoid doing the same.

b) Our professional education in counseling and resolving conflict compensated for our upbringing (our schooling included graduate study, theses, research and writing, internships, and workshops throughout our careers).

c) Having witnessed so much dysfunction within our families, we both made a conscious decision to not recreate the past—and it worked flawlessly.

d) None of the above.

If you chose anything but (d), you just flunked Relationships 101. But if you chose (b), know you aren't alone. Many people really do assume that mental health professionals have picture-perfect relationships. So, if you too believe that marriage counselors, psychologists, or psychotherapists are healthier than you are in the relationship department, I've got a secret to tell you: divorce statistics for some mental healthcare folk are just as high as they are for everyone else in the country. I know a number of mental health professionals who work with couples who have been married two, three, or even five times!

The general statistics for divorce suggest that one in two marriages will fall apart. Education and psychological awareness don't necessarily immunize couples against the suffering that relationship dysfunction can create. Understand that if you have been struggling with relationships, it's because they're tough stuff!

Why Can't Education Save a Relationship?

"The acorn doesn't fall far from the tree." "She's a chip off the old block. "Her father is a pretty tough nut to crack, and she's just like him." "Like mother, like daughter." "He's oblivious to what's really happening— just like his mother." "Like father, like son." "Her mother never trusted anyone, and neither does she." "That mom and son are two peas out of the same pod." Need I go on?

The factors that influence our ability to build healthy relationships go deeper than we think. The foundation we are standing on for creating loving, long-lasting intimate partnerships is built on generations of relationships that came before us. Dig around in the secrets in your own family closet, and I bet you'll discover that the relationship problems you are experiencing today have some deep roots.

Communication skills and relationship role modeling are passed down from generation to generation. Here's an example. My grandfather always used a bit of humor with my grandmother during their disagreements, joking about his "man way of thinking." When I overheard this as a child, I noticed that it seemed to soften any strong emotions my grandmother might be feeling. When I met Michael, his wit reminded me of my grandfather's, and this characteristic was part of the attraction. Initially, his funny remarks during a mild disagreement would calm me down. But over time I found myself feeling shut down by his excessive use of humor. Instead of saying anything about it, though, I responded as my grandmother had—by laughing and changing the subject. So these little disagreements were never resolved, and soon I was building one large, unspoken resentment. It's worthwhile to look back at these family patterns. Examining how our parents and grandparents solved disagreements or expressed displeasure with one another is not about placing blame. It's about exploring how we developed our communication behaviors.

Here's another brain teaser for you. During the early years of our relationship, what do you think Michael and I looked like when we did argue?

A Fight at the Brandon House

The scene takes place in the kitchen. The garbage disposal isn't working.

Michael: (*with a look of exasperation and a calm, parental tone*) I can't believe the garbage disposal is broken again. What did you put down the drain this time?

Carla: (*immediately defensive*) Why do you always assume it's my fault? I didn't put anything down the drain.

Michael: (*in an even monotone*) How many times have I had to fix this garbage disposal? When will you learn? Oh, well. I guess I'll just have to go spend money on a new one—again.

Carla: *(escalating into anger)* Why do you always have to blame me for everything? In your eyes everything is always my fault! You treat me like I'm responsible for every single thing that goes wrong around here!

Michael: *(calmly rinsing his hands and starting to clean up the mess in the sink)* I'm not going to talk to you when you act like this. You are overreacting and being very immature.

Carla: *(escalating into rage)* That's right. Acting like the martyr who always has to do the dirty work around here, like the poor victim married to this shrew of a wife who only creates problems for you.

Michael: *(casting a shaming look at Carla)* I'm going to finish cleaning this mess up and then go out to play golf. In the future, you need to think before you put something down the garbage disposal.

Carla: *(in a full-blown rage, smashing a sugar bowl to the floor)* I told you I didn't put anything down that damn drain! I haven't been home all day! Last night *you* cleaned up the dishes. I haven't touched that garbage disposal or the sink for twenty-four hours!

Michael: *(looking frightened and concerned)* Carla, you need to get a hold of yourself. All that I'm asking is that you stop putting stuff down the disposal. Now this discussion is over.

Carla: *(erupting with curses, then screaming)* That's right, I'm the idiot who can't do anything right and you're the saint, so I guess we will just bury this and not talk about it?

Michael walks out of the room, gathers up his golf clubs, and is out the door.

Carla: *(screaming, throwing a glass vase onto the floor)* I didn't do anything wrong!

She sits down on the floor and cries.

When Michael returns from the golf course, Carla is angrily slamming pans around in the kitchen, thinking about divorce and cooking dinner. Michael ignores her and retreats to the garage to repair a light fixture. Nothing more is discussed and the situation is never resolved.

• • •

Did either of us win that fight? I think not. I reacted to the situation like a card-carrying member of my family, with passion, violence, and rage. Feeling unappreciated and blamed, I got lost in emotion. So I couldn't take the action I needed to take to calmly state, "No, I didn't break the garbage disposal, I didn't put anything down the drain that wasn't supposed to be there, and I'm saddened and angry to hear you immediately blaming me for this. So I'm going to leave the room before I personalize this situation and lose my temper."

Michael, on the other hand, pulled back emotionally each time I raged. The louder I shouted, the more he withdrew. Eventually, he just shut me out and focused on fixing the disposal and cleaning up the mess. Feeling his emotional distance, I raged even more and became violent. Michael, in turn, found ways to occupy his mind to block out not only me but the tension that was flying through the air. The more he pushed me away, the more I reacted.

Did we make conscious decisions to react the way we did? Neither of us felt better afterward. Why couldn't we find and use better communication skills?

How We Learn about Relationships

In childhood we learn the basic components of both creating and maintaining relationships. Little girls learn about being female by watching their mothers and other female caretakers in the home. Young boys begin modeling the male traits exhibited by their fathers, grandfathers, uncles, and older brothers. Little girls fall in love for the first time with their fathers. They learn about how men treat women by playing out "in love" relationships with Daddy. Little boys want to marry Mom: they discover the roots of loving relationships between men and women by falling "in love" with their mommies. The above is a truism for both heterosexuals and homosexuals.

We learn about ourselves and our relationships with others by watching our parents' every move. We observe their behaviors, loving and otherwise; their likes and dislikes; their positive characteristics; their emotions and spirituality; their self-esteem and their self-hatred; their habits, prejudices, addictions, and survival skills. Unaddressed losses and traumas directly affect us as children and set the stage for us as adults. We can end up with behaviors and characteristics that are exclusively like Mom's or specifically like Dad's, but more often than not are a combination of the two. If we were not raised by our parents, we will be affected by the behaviors and characteristics of our primary caretakers. When a parent is absent, for whatever reason, that fact will affect our adult relationships. An absent parent leaves us without some of the modeling we need for communicating effectively. If a young boy loses his mother to an early death, as a grown man he might lack some of the skills needed to communicate intimately with women. Without daily interaction with his mother during his youth, his first safe female relationship, it becomes more difficult to learn those skills.

During childhood, we also observe how people within the family interact with each other and with us. We develop a foundation upon which all of our future relationships will be built. In other words, the family is a sort of "boot camp" training ground for the world of adult interactions. Understanding this is half the battle to conquering intimacy difficulties. Our intimacy trouble spots will interfere with honest communication, the skills to disagree or sort out differences with mutual respect, and the ability to hold on to who we are while in a relationship.

Asking the Right Questions

How often I hear, "My parents have been married for forty years and they've never had a fight! Why can't I have a long-term relationship like that?" The question should never be, "Why can't I have a long-term relationship like my parents'?" but instead, "What may I have learned from my parents' long-term relationship that might be making it difficult for me to have healthy relationships?"

Other clients of mine have said, "My parents hated each other. They drank too much, took too many pills, were unfaithful to each other, and were impossible to be around. The screaming was frightening. I keep trying to find a healthy partner, but I seem to always pick losers. Why do I keep recreating my parents' madness?" Instead of asking, "Why do I keep attracting bad relationships?" we really need to ask, "What's so attractive and familiar to me about these destructive relationships?"

Most of us who suffer from relationship disappointment have been asking the wrong questions for years. Michael and I almost ended our marriage because we didn't know how to ask the right questions. Instead we focused on the blame game and each others' behaviors and kept expecting change. Each of us thought, "If my partner would just see the light and change, all would be well!" Eventually we discovered this was not the solution.

So let's explore how we learned about relationships, and let's begin by asking the right questions. But before doing so let's remember that the purpose of the Right Questions exercise is not to blame those who raised us during our childhood. If you have anger toward your parents or caregivers, know this we will address those issues soon. For now we are just gathering facts and examining the relationship information our parents, grandparents, and caretakers have passed on to us either knowingly or unknowingly.

Understanding Your Personal History:
The First Step to Healing

To fully understand how our history has impacted our current relationship difficulties, we might need to ask ourselves some very specific questions. Such questions can be found in the chapter 2 worksheet in appendix A at the back of this book. I suggest you look at them now at least briefly, then, after you've finished reading the rest of this book, thoroughly explore them on paper.

Through answering these questions you will learn a great deal about how you've interacted with present and past partners. Taking the time to really analyze our relationships can move unconscious reactions and behavior to awareness. When we are more aware, we can then take steps to make changes.

By completing these exercises, you will be taking a tremendous step toward understanding not only yourself and your partner or partners, but how you learned about relationships. If the information you have gathered feels overwhelming, consider getting some help: visit with a therapist, talk to a clergyperson, attend a Twelve Step meeting, or find a self-help group in your community that discusses interpersonal relationship issues. You don't have to do this alone! When we have an honest appraisal of the relationship values, communication skills, and troubleshooting abilities of those who came before us, we will better understand our own foundation for healthy intimacy. By honestly taking stock of our relationship today, we can then make positive decisions about how we behave with our partner.

Where to Go from Here

Reviewing or actually doing the worksheet exercises can help you begin to ask the right questions about your present or past partner and your relationship with this person. You may also begin to see that your partner has or had characteristics similar to one or both of your parents'. Possibly you've had to go back a generation to your grandparents to find these similarities. Maybe you have discovered that you have recreated the dynamics of your parents' relationship within your own intimate connections. Or you have found that the secrets in your family have some how impacted your communication skills and ability to problem solve with your partner.

Maybe your own unresolved childhood hurt has been affecting your relationships. Possibly you've discovered that you aren't a very good judge of character when it comes to choosing a partner, or that you're clueless about navigating relationship challenges. Or that although you've been blaming your partner for the downfall of your relationship, you have enabled unacceptable behavior by not setting limits, saying no, or standing up for yourself. In other words, you have discovered you are part of the problem.

If you're feeling a little confused, don't be surprised. This new information can leave us feeling overwhelmed and a bit rattled! More clarity is just around the corner, and it will smooth out any of the edginess you may be experiencing. And be aware of that feeling confused is a good sign: it means you don't have all the answers and you're open to learning.

Now that you have some insight on how your family upbringing prepared you for relationships, it's time to take a closer look at a few specific problem areas couples often confront. Not all of these issues will fit for you, but I suspect some will. Recognize that you have started to rebuild a foundation for yourself, one that will enable you to eventually experience healthy relationships. The following chapters will add strength to your foundation. As we move into the next part of this book, continue to be willing to learn and to keep an open mind.

• • •

3

Painful Memories:
The Impact of Childhood Abuse
on Healthy Intimacy

*Love is a fire. But whether it is going to warm your hearth or burn
down your house, you can never tell.*

— JOAN CRAWFORD, HOLLYWOOD LEGEND ACCUSED BY HER DAUGHTER OF CHILD ABUSE

Hurricane Ike was churning in the Gulf of Mexico and there was a high probability that twenty-foot waves would be soaking my backyard in a day or two. My clients were nervously canceling their appointments, so I was surprised to see Judith sitting in my office. Her attention was totally focused on the pages of a book balanced on her knees. "What are you reading?" I asked. As she slowly closed the thick paperback, I recognized a picture of sultry actress Joan Crawford on the front cover.

Seeing the photograph of the star reminded me of my own youth. As a young girl I'd been frightened out of my wits by Crawford's portrayal of the demonic sister in the classic thriller *Whatever Happened to Baby Jane?* Sadly, the actress's incredible performance had paralleled her own painful, erratic, disturbing, life. Off-screen allegations of alcoholism, raging behavior, and violence eventually tainted her stellar professional reputation. After Crawford's death, her adopted daughter wrote a biography describing her as a less-than-perfect mother.

In 1978, when Christina Crawford published her tell-all account of her troubled childhood, most of the public still believed child abuse didn't happen in the mansions of the rich and famous. Titled *Mommie Dearest,* the tragic Hollywood exposé shattered that myth and caused a stir in a business where image is everything. Though several siblings disputed the disturbing recollections Christina publicly disclosed, famous contemporaries of the family, such as June Allyson, Helen Hayes, and even Bette Davis, verified the sad stories. The distressing tales of abuse in Christina Crawford's book were obviously triggering feelings for Judith.

The wind outside was blowing hard, and Judith was working just as hard at controlling her internal storm of emotion. Judith had initially come to see me because of concerns about her relationships. Now in her thirties, she had spent years going from one unsuccessful love affair to the next. Realizing she was beginning to sound just like her mother during disagreements with partners, she feared something in her childhood was creating problems for her.

During her initial session she told me, "My mother was a complaining shrew, and I don't want to be like her. Finally, I'm dating someone I really care about and I don't want this relationship to end like all the rest." More concerning were her issues around sex. "Sex always becomes a serious problem after I've been in a relationship for two or three months," she said. "For the first several weeks lovemaking is great, but then I suddenly shut down sexually. I can't figure out how to change this pattern and I feel so stuck." Judith briefly explored some of her sad childhood history, which included her father's alcoholism, but like so many survivors of abuse she'd become frustrated. She had trouble recalling most of her youth, so she couldn't see how her childhood was related to her relationship problems.

Sitting down in my rocking chair, I asked, "Did you know that Joan Crawford was married four times and divorced three of her husbands? And I've read she'd had sexual affairs with both men and women, including an alleged one-night stand with Marilyn Monroe!" Judith looked surprised. "Pretty wild stuff, isn't it?" I added. Picking up the book and looking at Crawford's porcelain skin, luscious lashes, and full lips, I continued, "Sadly, this incredibly gifted actress suffered a great deal of trauma in her youth, and I suspect she never healed from it. Booze, excessive sexual acting out, fame, fortune, and the love of six adopted children couldn't erase her pain." Sighing, I added, "I've often wondered if she ever really knew just how talented she was."

Like Crawford, Judith was a very successful woman who continually questioned her own abilities. In the past she'd used alcohol and prescription drugs to mask her feelings. As her addictions worsened, her ability to perform in her job was compromised, and she started making major mistakes. One serious error in judgment had cost her thousands of dollars, and it was this bad business deal that had finally landed her in a detox unit.

By the time Judith arrived at my office, she'd been abstinent from her addictions for more than a decade. Since beginning recovery, this incredibly bright woman had been able to reestablish herself in her business and quickly made her mark in her profession. Well respected by her community, she'd even become involved in city politics. Judith and I spent several sessions discussing her inability to enjoy her accomplishments. She had difficulty accepting her success and continued to suffer from free-floating anxiety, a lack of self-confidence, and a deep sense of emptiness.

Handing *Mommie Dearest* back to her, I said, "The tragic accounts of Joan Crawford abusing her children physically and emotionally are well known. But most of the public is unaware that she too was a victim of serious trauma. To start with, during her marriage to movie star Franchot Tone she suffered severe domestic violence. And she had two heart-wrenching miscarriages."

Surprised, Judith replied, "That's terrible. I just saw her as an abusive mother and spoiled celebrity. Who'd have thought this wealthy, glamorous woman had suffered so much pain herself?" A bolt of lightning shot across the darkening sky, quickly followed by a clap of thunder. After closing the window blinds. I turned to Judith and added, "Yes, appearances can be deceiving, and it gets even worse. Her youth was even more distressing."

Many celebrities endure horrific emotional, physical, or even sexual abuse during their younger years. It isn't a mistake they end up in Hollywood, the land of make-believe and pretend. Youngsters who are traumatized often call on their imaginations and take on new personalities to survive. Joan Crawford's sad story isn't that unusual. Her parents were believed to have had a very troubled relationship and supposedly divorced before or shortly after her birth. Interestingly, the legality of their marriage has been questioned. At that time, being born out of wedlock or seen as illegitimate would have created a great deal of shame. Her mother cleaned houses to put food on the table, and young Joan swore she would never mop or scrub floors.

Though her mother eventually remarried, this union also ended in divorce. Alleged to have associations with organized crime, Crawford's stepfather was put on trial for embezzlement. He too eventually ended up walking out on the family. At the time, the future actress was just ten years old. Abandonment by her father and then a stepfather must have set her up to carry a tremendous sense of hurt, anger, and mistrust toward men.

Crawford's mother had her fair share of personal difficulties and was most likely burdened with unresolved grief, emotional pain, and loss. Not only did she divorce twice, her oldest daughter, Daisy, died shortly before Joan was born. When a parent doesn't grieve, the unaddressed emotions trickle down to the children. Youngsters will absorb the feelings their parents ignore or try to push aside. Joan most likely felt her mother's sadness, and this in turn set her up for her own future battles with depression. Crawford's incredible acting abilities definitely appear to be rooted in a great deal of early hardship.

According to her daughter's book, the successful actress dealt with her own sense of loss and sadness by raging. Many people suffering from depression periodically react with violent angry outbursts, and there's actually a cycle to this behavior. The adrenaline produced from rage acts physiologically as a sort of temporary antidepressant. After a depressed person blows up, adrenaline flows throughout the body and the mood improves. But this emotional elevator works only temporarily, and with time untreated depression returns. As it deepens, another violent outburst will occur and the cycle begins again. This process is unconsious, and for children living with an adult caught up in this emotionally addictive behavior, the repercussions can be devastating.

"Judith?" I asked. "Who do you identify with more in the book? The rageful alcoholic actress Joan or the abused and neglected daughter Christina?" After thinking for a few moments she replied, "Both. On the one hand, I grew up with a mother who was angry and depressed all the time. I never knew if she was going to explode with rage or threaten suicide. My father was a good-looking alcoholic who loved vodka and the ladies, and I know my mother was furious about this. I remember lying in bed trying to sleep, only to have her burst into my room in the middle of the night in a rage about my father." Shaking her head, she added, "I haven't thought of that in years."

I could tell Judith's emotional dam was cracking. She was remembering traumatic events that had been buried for decades. "So," I asked, "you related to the mother's raging behavior as described by the daughter?" With this, a few tears trickled down Judith's cheeks as she nodded yes. Then I asked, "Do you know that being exposed to your mother's constant explosive raging was a form of emotional abuse, while hearing about your father's sexual affairs was actually sexually abusive?" Judith shook her head no and the tears came faster.

It was time to connect all the dots, so I added, "Children who grow up in families like yours often have extreme difficulties in their adult relationships. Watching your parents refuse to resolve their issues or take responsibility for their actions—that set you up for relationship problems too. Your chances for an intimate partnership have always been compromised because neither of your parents modeled for you what healthy intimacy looks like. Instead, they covered up their pain with addiction, never took the steps necessary to help themselves, and blamed each other for their unhappiness. How are you supposed to know how to problem-solve with a partner if you've never been exposed to this?"

As painful as this realization was, Judith was starting to grasp how her childhood abuse had set her up to fail in her relationships, so I continued. "Your father avoided dealing with his feelings by engaging in a series of extramarital affairs. Sex altered his mood as effectively as a tall glass of whisky would for an alcoholic. Your mother was a rager who altered her mood with adrenaline. Instead of seeking appropriate help for her adult situation, she dumped it on you. How could you be a kid when your parent was so needy of your emotional support? And if you constantly heard your mother complain about sex while your father was sexually irresponsible, how could you ever develop a healthy concept of sex?" This connection surprised Judith, but she definitely understood it.

Judith's eyes were red-rimmed; she was finally feeling her feelings about her youth. "As a direct result of your history, you don't have all the tools you need to work through relationship problems," I went on. "You don't know how to sustain healthy intimacy because you never had that with either of your parents. Your childhood was unpredictable, frightening, and dysfunctional. This doesn't mean your parents didn't love you. What it does mean is that they were two damaged people who didn't have the health they needed to successfully parent you. You haven't resolved these issues, so your traumatic history is interfering with your ability to enjoy long-term emotional and sexual intimacy in your relationships."

Judith sobbed her eyes out for about fifteen minutes. After I gave her the last tissue I had, she wiped her face and asked, "Can I have a healthy relationship with the new guy in my life? Or will I scare him off like all the rest?" Seeing the willingness she had to do whatever it took to heal herself, I replied, "Right now your history rules your life and dictates your behavior in your relationships. Your destructive patterns are a direct result of your painful past. These patterns of behavior or survival skills took great care of you during your childhood. Today, they're no longer working for you. No matter how hard you try to ignore your past, sweep your traumas under the rug, or minimize the impact of your abuse, the emotions related to your difficult childhood will always there. Once you look your abuse squarely in the eye, feel all feelings associated with this period in your life, and slowly release these emotions, not only will you begin to remember more of your childhood, but you'll be set free from your own destructive patterns of behavior. Also, separating your parents' ideas about sexuality from how you see yourself as sexual being today will improve your sex life. With this, you'll finally be able to have a truly intimate relationship."

The weather outside was quickly getting worse, and when the lights started to flicker I knew lightning had struck a transformer. Before the lights went out for good, it was time to end the session and leave the office. As we made our way out into the wind and rain, Judith popped open her pink umbrella, gave me a quick hug, and said, "I finally feel hopeful!"

Getting to the Roots of Intimacy Difficulties

When we have disagreements with our partners, who are we really at odds with? If we're having sexual difficulty, what's at the root of it? Are our issues with our mates really about here-and-now problems, or are they unresolved difficulties from the past? What we really afraid of? Is it our partner, or is it someone who hurt us deeply long ago?

Past traumas affect our ability to trust, connect, and feel safe with another human being. Such difficult experiences may involve a troubled childhood, unresolved hurts with parents, old wounds such as a rape or physical abuse, or previous traumatic relationships or love affairs. Many of us suffer serious relationship difficulties but then refuse to look for the origins of these troubles. Breezing over these issues with a feel-good approach—whether it's overreliance on short-term therapy, life coaching, or a superficial weekend workshop—won't resolve them. The hurt, shame, anger, fear, and grief are too deep. We need to love ourselves enough to spend the time needed to heal from these losses. If we understand how they influence our relationships today, we have a starting point for healing intimacy difficulties. So let's take a look at what unresolved trauma looks like.

Trauma comes in a variety of forms, but to simplify matters let's focus on child abuse (much of this information can also be applied to other instances of trauma). Most violence against children takes place within the family unit, but it also occurs outside of the system. There are even instances of children being traumatized for years while parents remain completely unaware of it. Review the following list of abuses to see if any of these examples are similar to what you or your partner may have experienced.

General Safety (Physical and Emotional)

- Neglect, emotional abandonment, or lack of nurturing
- Being deprived of basic needs such as nutritious food, clothing, shelter, and healthy touch
- Exposure to unsafe environments and people, including care-givers who abuse substances
- Poor boundaries with regard to home routines such as bedtime (for example, because of parental addictions)
- No medical attention when sick; no routine doctor, dentist, and eye care visits
- Exposure to excessive raging by a parent or caregiver
- Being bullied by adults, or threatened by other children and then not protected by adults
- Being hurt in any way, then being instructed to not tell anyone about it
- Being used as a go-between when parents are separating or divorced; being told by one parent to lie about the other
- Losing a parent or sibling to death and not receiving proper emotional support
- Physical abandonment by parents or caregivers

Physical Violence

- Being subjected to excessive slapping, pushing, or shaking
- Being kicked and/or beaten, with or without implements
- Being subjected to inappropriate physical procedures such as excessive enemas

Sexual Violence
- Acts of rape or sexual molestation inside or outside the home: for example, by relatives, babysitters, older neighborhood children, or strangers
- Being forced to touch someone in a sexual manner or perform any sexual act
- Exposure by an older person to adult sexual activities, such as pornography, sexual acts or games, strip joints, or prostitution
- Living with caretakers who behave inappropriately sexually or talk too openly about their sexual habits
- Being the victim of a voyeuristic adult
- Inappropriate touching, hugging, kissing, or dancing with an older person (activities that feel wrong or scary)
- Being sexually penetrated in any manner (not including medical exams, although even those must be handled properly to avoid psychological discomfort)

If the situation isn't intervened upon and resolved, traumatized children naturally develop survival skills that can be self-destructive. And they keep using them both consciously and unconsciously into adulthood. These abuse-related coping behaviors interfere with healthy choice-making, setting up even more difficulties. Most abuse survivors aren't even aware they have choices in how they act or respond, especially when it comes to relationships.

Reactions to Abuse

Over the course of a lifetime, what are some common reactions to child abuse? Read the list below and see if you can relate to any of these symptoms.

ADDICTIVE BEHAVIORS

Addiction to mood-altering chemical substances, food, sex, or repetitive obsessive-compulsive behaviors is common among survivors of abuse;

many use prescription and over-the-counter medications and alcohol or illegal drugs to cope with emotions related to the trauma. Food-addicted survivors will eat when not hungry or when confronted with frustration, loneliness, grief, fear, or depression, or they may engage in bulimia, anorexia, or compulsive exercise. Eating only certain types of foods (such as health foods or organic products) can become obsessive. When our life rotates around our eating patterns, we don't have time to feel the emotions related to our trauma. Like addictions, obsessive-compulsive behaviors, including repetitive ones, serve to block out feelings.

In the very short term, addictions work well to temporarily blunt the emotions and distance survivors from the feelings associated with the abuse. Unfortunately, the consequences of any addiction are severe difficulties in many realms: physical, professional, legal, social, and personal, including intimate relationships.

CONCERNING BEHAVIORS

These self-destructive behaviors, ranging from mild to severe, often indicate a preoccupation or major concern. During childhood, excessive bedwetting may occur. Other signs, at various ages, include scab picking, pulling hair out of the head, eyelash pulling, nail biting, and excessive tattooing. Of particular concern is cutting, but self-mutilation in any form into adulthood can indicate a possible abuse history.

DESTRUCTIVE BEHAVIORS

Some survivors develop a history of destructive acting out with property or behaving disrespectfully or even violently toward others. As children or teens, some are fascinated with hurting or killing animals or setting fires. Pleasure may be taken in discussing these activities.

DISSOCIATION

One very common sign of past unresolved trauma is difficulty feeling connected with others and events in one's environment. Survivors may report feeling emotionally "checked out," or constantly distracted, forgetful, or foggy. Conversations are forgotten, appointments are missed, and personal items are easily lost.

DISTORTED PERCEPTION OF THE PHYSICAL, EMOTIONAL, OR SOCIAL SELF

Survivors often have an inaccurate perception of the self or an intense dislike of the physical body. Feeling inadequate and unlikable and reacting with hostility toward the self is not unusual. They may have a strong need to be the center of attention, to prove that "I'm okay and likeable."

EXCESSIVE FANTASY

Some trauma survivors drift frequently into daydreams; they may live in an emotional fantasy, at times confusing it with reality. They may escape through fantasy in books, movies, or television to avoid being emotionally present; they may excessively play video games or use other electronic gadgets.

INAPPROPRIATE AFFECT

Trauma survivors are often out of touch with their feelings. Not knowing how to cry or feel anger at appropriate times, trauma survivors may overreact to a variety of situations, including harmless comments, constructive criticism, or healthy touch from others. Movies may spark a big reaction, and authority figures may seem threatening. The survivor's excessive tears, rage, or fear can often baffle others. Underreaction is also common and can be a result of trauma.

INAPPROPRIATE BOUNDARIES

Many trauma survivors don't know how to protect themselves from hurtful people or potentially dangerous situations. They can be overly trusting and when confronted with offenders will feel frozen, numb, or frightened. They may hidebehind walls of rage, fear, or shame to isolate or avoid others—which can also set up a sense of loneliness. When feeling vulnerable or threatened, the person may act out in antisocial ways. Another common sign is an overwhelming fear of being out of control.

INAPPROPRIATE SEXUAL ACTING OUT

Signs include sexual addiction, infidelity, difficulty maintaining long-term sexual relationships, a constant need for outside sexual stimulation to achieve an orgasm, abuse of sexually enhancing medications or herbal supplements, and confusing sex with intimacy and love.

INAPPROPRIATE SEXUAL BOUNDARIES

Some survivors discuss sexual matters too openly, engage in sexually acting out when they don't want to or can't say no to sexual advances, and may be unaware when their clothing is too tight, revealing, or otherwise inappropriate. Some have difficulty recognizing when they're sending the wrong message to people who may see their behavior as an invitation for sex or connection.

NIGHT TERRORS OR OTHER SLEEP DISORDERS

Many abuse survivors suffer from sleep disorders because they have difficulty feeling safe at night. To cope with this, they may use sleep medications or herbs to excess; some feel a need for extra pillows or blankets to cover up with. They may not feel safe sleeping with a partner; or they may follow rigid nighttime rituals with regard to sleeping behavior in general.

NOT NOTICING PHYSICAL PAIN

Many abuse survivors are out of touch with the body's need for food, rest, and healthy touch. In some cases, they may not notice or feel physical pain during or after an injury.

OUT-OF-BODY SENSATION

Trauma survivors often report a feeling of being disconnected from the physical self. This form of dissociation—the sensation of literally floating out of the body—can be a strong indication of unresolved trauma or abuse.

OVERWHELMING SENSE OF SHAME

Another common sign is a feeling of inadequacy with a strong need to cover up normal imperfections. Many abuse survivors fear others will find out their secrets, and they often feel that their life is a fraud. Because of a strong need for control and perfection, many abuse survivors can't handle constructive suggestions. Some survivors will abuse diets, gym workouts, and plastic surgery, pursuing these to excess.

PANIC OR ANXIETY ATTACKS (CONSEQUENCES OF FEELING OUT OF CONTROL)

Symptoms of a panic or anxiety attack include hyperventilating, or difficulty breathing; upset stomach or nausea; wanting to hide and isolate; feeling dizzy or hot; and feeling close to passing out. People having a panic attack are forced to stop what they are doing and remove themselves from whatever people, places, or situations feel unsafe and out of their control. Usually, these people, places, or situations are triggering unresolved emotions tied to an early trauma. Panic attacks force a "time out."

PHOBIAS, OVERWHELMING FEARS

Abuse trauma survivors are often left feeling powerless—which can lead to intense fears of particular types of people, places, or things. Some examples: excessive fear of crowds, doctors, dentists, animals, germs, or flying. Such phobias can trigger feelings of being out of control—a state that can actually feel like dying, for abuse survivors out of touch or unresolved with their painful history.

PHYSICAL OR PSYCHOSOMATIC DIFFICULTIES

Survivors of trauma often report numerous psychosomatic or real illnesses, such as excessive urinary tract infections starting at an early age, gastrointestinal difficulties, migraine headaches, insomnia, and vaginal or bladder infections. Other physical issues that may surface from time to time are allergies, rashes, teeth grinding, muscle tremors, breathing problems, body tics, and pain in the genital, pelvic, or abdominal regions. Even though the memory of a traumatic experience may retreat underground into unconsciousness, the feelings may continually resurface psychosomatically.

SENSE OF REPEATED VICTIMIZATION

Though most survivors are too trusting at times, they can also be highly untrustful, sometimes suddenly. Some abuse survivors become overly cautious and suspicious of others and their motives. Feeling taken advantage of, scapegoated, ridiculed, or misunderstood, they may believe the world is a dangerous, unfair place.

SEXUAL ANOREXIA

Sexuality with sexual avoidance can become an issue for abuse survivors. As the anorexic rejects food, the sexual anorexic will avoid or purposefully abstain from sexually connecting with another person. Certain sex acts, even common ones, can cause extreme emotional or even physical discomfort—possibly resulting in frigidity, inability to reach orgasm, or impotence with no physiological basis. If sex in a relationship is similar to the molestation experienced in childhood, the survivor may distance from sexual contact, or, conversely, may insist on that type of sex act in order to reach orgasm. Some survivors of abuse eventually find sex with self more acceptable than sex with another person.

UNEXPLAINED DEPRESSIONS

Survivors of abuse regularly report feeling low, sad, or down for unexplained reasons. In such cases, medication for depression usually doesn't provide long-term results. They may isolate and withdraw from group or family activities; when they feel threatened emotionally or physically, they may act out with hostility or rage.

These reactions to abuse can occur even if the survivor has no memories of the trauma. Many people with a painful history don't have conscious recall because they've repressed their memories of trauma. In this way they distance themselves from the abuse emotionally, but when they find themselves depressed or acting out in a relationship, survivors don't know why. Partners often feel as though the survivor is responding like this on purpose: *If she really loved me, she'd change,* or *He just doesn't see how his behavior is hurting me.* Abuse reactions acted out in a relationship typically aren't intentional. That's why it's so important for survivors to take responsibility and get honest about the impact their histories have had on them. Only in this way can such unconscious reactions become conscious and then disentangled from the relationship. And this disentangling can be done even when there is memory loss about the trauma.

Abuse Reactions in Relationships

In severely dysfunctional relationships affected by unresolved trauma, I have found that abuse survivors tend to fit into one of two personality types: Closed Book and Open Book. In the former, emotional unavailability is often a big concern; in the latter, emotions may fly too furiously to partners to follow. Let's take a closer look at these two types—keeping in mind that these are generalizations, and that some people may mix the two types.

The Closed Book Personality Type

For a Closed Book type, the survivor's fear of abandonment sets the stage for emotional distancing. Typically such a person comes from a family setting where they've learned to turn off their emotions, avoid vulnerability, and protect themselves from potential hurt. Now, even in adulthood, the person operates from the deep-seated, often unconscious core belief: "If I shut you out emotionally, I'm not at risk of feeling abandoned if you should leave me or hurt me in any way." Of course this belief isn't a purposeful one; it's a by-product of growing up in a home where it was never safe to be a needy child. Closed Books usually seem very much in control, and they're often not seen as suffering from past abuse. But looks can be utterly deceiving.

See if you or your partner has any of the following characteristics:

- Closed Books don't easily trust others; instead they emotionally isolate themselves, tend to keep secrets, and rarely share how they really feel.

- They present a public side, which is on display most of the time, and they see being vulnerable as an invitation for exploitation or abuse.

- They may be defensive when others express concern about their behavior, or they may deny, deflect, turn the tables, and blame others when confronted. ("You're saying I'm difficult to get along with? Well, what about you? You have difficulties with everyone!")

- They approach relationships with mistrust and tend to believe that everyone has a hidden agenda.

- When feeling too much intimacy or closeness, they may react with

49

distancing behavior, pulling away emotionally or even physically.

- They share only those opinions that they believe are acceptable.

- When a partner comes too close—with confrontation, constructive suggestions, or even simply care and concern—they may distance themselves with punishing silence, shaming comments, or physical withdrawal.

- They may empower others with compliments to deflect attention from themselves.

- Closed Books need to be in control of themselves and others, and their environment and life must be predictable and orderly.

We can learn to lower our walls and experience vulnerability in a relationship only if we're willing to explore why we need these rigid boundaries in the first place. When we understand that we survived our trauma by distancing ourselves from the pain, anger, and shame we didn't know how to feel at the time, we can begin reclaiming our emotional self. Without emotions, we can't rely on our perceptions of what we feel, hear, or see. If we can't develop healthy insight and awareness untainted by our trauma, we can't build healthy boundaries. By looking at our history and finally feeling the emotions we have avoided for so many years, we can begin letting others into our lives. Once we do this, we can start to experience healthy intimacy. The process of healing is slow and scary at times, but with patience we can replace our brick walls with flexible boundaries and loving relationships.

The Open Book Personality Type

Interestingly, people who are Closed Books often hook up with over-feeling, boundary-less Open Book types. Working with persons who have absolutely no boundaries at all is like dealing with a Texas tornado. The emotions swing from one extreme to the other, reactions are unpredictable, and these people often don't know how to censor themselves when it's in their own best interest. Open Book trauma survivors often endured abuse by being too gullible and unquestioning. They never developed the ability to maintain their own reality; instead they easily accept the perceptions of others. As children they needed to constantly take the emotional temperature of everyone around them, and did so by keeping their boundaries porous. Their survival depended upon knowing without being told when Dad was going to blow up and throw dishes across the room, or when Mom had been drinking. Each of us has the gift of intuition, but when we grow up in a chaotic environment we almost have to become psychic in order to predict what will happen next! Without filters or boundaries children are able to do this.

Trying to guess with 100-percent accuracy what crisis will take place next keeps the adrenaline pumping. Open Books learn to be on alert at all times, and as adults the addiction to constant chaos continues. Open Books tend to seek out Closed Books because they appear to be stable and calm—but then when they don't react with intensity and high emotion, the Open Book is frustrated. Let's consider some characteristics of trauma survivors who are Open Book type personalities:

- Open Books tend to rescue and enable others, using this pattern to pump adrenaline and distract from taking care of their own needs.

- They are often not good judges of character and feel confused when they're taken advantage of.

- They tend to give of the self in excess, and the recipient of their giving is often an offender personality who isn't appreciative.

- They often feel uncomfortable saying no to the demands of partners, family, friends, children, and peers. They are easily made to feel guilty.

- They often sacrifice their needs for the wants of others and then feel taken advantage of, unacknowledged, used, or abused.

- They can appear to be good listeners and often ask too many personal questions because they're unable to censor themselves. Being gullible, they rarely question what they're told and tend to believe everything they hear.

- They tend to overreact to certain situations with extreme emotion, and then question why others aren't responding as they are.

- They may "tell all" without thinking about the possible consequences, and are then surprised when what they share is used against them.

- They accept unacceptable behavior from others in order to avoid rejection.

An Open Book lacking in boundaries will feel the emotions a Closed Book is ignoring. Open Books can overwhelm partners by overreacting to situations and by dramatizing. If we're an Open Book, we need to examine why we developed such porous boundaries as children, and how the chaos of our youth has hurt us. The pain an Open Book experienced during childhood is easily triggered by partners and the environment so it's important to resolve our old wounds. Once we do this, we're less likely to feel so triggered by our mate's emotions. When Open Books stop soaking up all of the emotions in a relationship, Closed Books then have to begin taking responsibility for their own feelings.

I'm an Open Book and Michael is a Closed Book. Our healing as a couple required both of us to individually explore old unresolved traumas that were complicating intimacy issues in our relationship. Once we'd done this, we then came together as a couple to develop rules that would help us establish healthy boundaries to live by as a couple.

Healthy intimacy requires a great deal of work. Jumping ship when in a troubled relationship, believing separation from a particular person is the solution, rarely solves long-term intimacy issues. Believing that we've played no part in the relationship dysfunction is dishonest. A new lover will eventually fill the shoes of the previous mate. Moving from one marriage or affair to another, refusing to see how past unresolved traumas are responsible for our intimacy difficulties, will keep us locked in a cycle of relationship unhappiness.

If we are in a long-term dysfunctional relationship and settling for the way things are, we need to recognize we aren't doing ourself or our partner any favors. Keeping busy, hiding behind addictions or compulsions, and finding distractions to avoid confronting a lack of intimacy are sad ways to go through life. We don't have to be lonely with our partner. We can learn how to resolve differences. For healing to begin, each person must examine any past unresolved history of pain, hurt, loss, or abuse. Both need to stop focusing on one another and look to themselves instead. Distracting with the blame game only keeps us from healing our own pain. Resolution of unresolved traumas must be the first task we tackle. A relationship is a partnership, and neither person is totally responsible for all its grief and resentment. As I said to Michael many years ago, "If you're so doggone healthy, why on earth did you hook up with a nut like me?"

My hope is that you will have the courage to begin your own personal journey of self-discovery, whether or not your partner chooses to follow. If you don't have a relationship now, and you believe a new romance will complete you, think again. Heal yourself before you go looking for love, and then you will find true intimacy.

· · ·

4

The Emotional Affair: Cheating without the Sex

She is such a sad soul. It is good that it is over.
Nobody was happy anyway. I know I should preach
family love and unity, but in their case . . .

— MOTHER TERESA, ON THE DIVORCE OF CHARLES AND DIANA

"I'm not having sex with her! What more can I say? Why won't you listen to reason?" Eddie was furious, and for a few seconds I held my breath, wondering whether he would lose it all together and really start yelling. Glancing over at Michael, who was acting as co-therapist for this session, I could tell he had the same concern. The confrontation between our two clients was heating up, and we both knew it was time for us to just sit back for a bit.

Moving Robin and Eddie toward honestly looking at their relationship had proven to be more difficult than walking through setting concrete. With both of them stuck in so much emotional muck, exposing the buried relationship resentment was a real challenge. Finally, they were gaining some traction and stepping out of the sludge. This confrontation had been in the making for some time and it wasn't going to be easy for either of them. On the outside, Robin tried to maintain a cool-as-a-cucumber look, but I could see it was just a front because she was viciously picking at her cuticles. She had difficulty standing up to Eddie, who always turned every disagreement into a four-part mini-series. The more Eddie yelled, the more withdrawn Robin became.

Robin and Eddie had been living together for almost a year. They weren't married, but they'd agreed to be monogamous. During individual therapy sessions with me, Robin had worked on gathering up the courage to ask Eddie whether he was having a sexual affair with a woman who was part of their social group. Her concern had grown gradually. When they first moved in together, Robin and Eddie had had a great time setting up their townhouse, shopping for furniture, cooking meals, entertaining, and waking up every morning together in the same bed. But after five months of domestic bliss, Robin began to feel as though the honeymoon was over. Eddie wasn't as attentive as he'd once been, sex dropped off, and she found herself eating a number of her meals alone. Robin also noticed that Eddie was away from home more often than usual and frequently was with their friend Maggie.

Robin and Eddie had met Maggie and Bob when they joined a local sailing club. The two couples hit it off and began spending a great deal of time together. Afternoon barbeques, evening movies, weekend camping, and dinner at each other's homes became regular activities. That summer they'd sailed to Mexico and the following fall to Jamaica. Both Eddie and Robin had looked up to Maggie and Bob because they appeared to have a very close, loving relationship. The two had been married seven years, and Bob was always hugging Maggie and giving her kisses. He told anyone who would listen that he was the luckiest guy in the world because he was married to such a wonderful, beautiful, giving, sexy woman. Eddie would often say to Robin, "I hope we're as happy as they are after we've been together that long." Bob and Maggie appeared to be the perfect couple, but those hugs and kisses didn't tell the whole story.

Eddie and Robin were shocked when they learned Bob was sleeping with a coworker from his office. He told Eddie about the extramarital affair shortly after the sailing trip to Jamaica. When Eddie asked, "Are you going to tell Maggie?" Bob chuckled and said, "I really don't believe she ever needs to know. It isn't that serious. I still love Maggie." Eddie then shared the sad news with Robin, who asked, "Bob isn't going to tell his wife he's been having sex with another woman? And we're supposed to keep the secret and act as if nothing is wrong?" Shaking her head, she added, "Eventually she'll figure it out. She's not that dumb. I certainly would."

After that, Eddie and Robin socialized very little with Maggie and Bob. For a few weeks Maggie continued to be unaware of her husband's infidelity, but eventually she did find out. At a Christmas party she found Bob and the female coworker locking lips in the office kitchen. After that she immediately called Eddie in tears with the news.

For the next several months Robin was supportive of Eddie when he said he was having lunch with Maggie, or if he needed to excuse himself to take a phone call from her. She also knew Maggie was e-mailing Eddie and that she often text-messaged him several times a day. Sometimes hysterical telephone calls came in the middle of the night and if Robin answered the phone, she would gently awaken Eddie. Initially, she felt sorry for her friend Maggie. After a few months, Robin felt Eddie was taking too much time away from their relationship to attend to Maggie. Robin found herself resenting the fact that so much of their schedule rotated around Maggie's mood swings. She started to wonder when this pattern would end.

One day, Robin saw Bob at the grocery store, and when she asked him how he was doing, he told her his affair with his coworker had ended. He added that he was sorry he'd expected her and Eddie to carry the secret about his affair and keep it hidden from Maggie. Then Bob surprised Robin by telling her there'd been lots of problems in the marriage and he'd used the affair to get out of it. When Robin said, "That's really twisted, Bob," he agreed with her and then said he was in counseling. Robin then told Bob that Eddie was spending a lot of time with Maggie because she was still very upset. With this, Bob gave her a hug, shook his head, and said, "You'd better watch that man of yours." Leaving the store, Robin thought, "What did that mean? I wonder what's really going on between those two."

Early one morning the phone ran again. It was a weepy Maggie asking for Eddie. After giving him a hard push, Robin handed him the telephone, rolled over, and wondered why Maggie never wanted to talk to her. Why did she always insist on talking to Eddie? Wasn't she her friend too? Hadn't she let Maggie disrupt her life long enough? She and Bob had split up more than three months ago. Why was Eddie spending even more time with her? If anything, Maggie seemed to be even more demanding of Eddie's time now than before.

One Saturday afternoon, Robin and Eddie were getting ready to go to a neighboring town to pick up their new puppy. As she dressed, Robin thought to herself, *A day without Maggie!* For several months they'd researched dog breeds and breeders and had finally decided on a golden retriever. Picking out cute names, searching for the perfect doggie bed, and playing with puppy toys had been great fun. Robin had even noticed Eddie was spending more time at home. That day, both of them were looking forward to bringing their new furry family member home. *Finally,* she said to herself, *we're becoming a real couple again.*

As they drove away, Eddie's cell phone began to ring and Robin lifted it to look at the caller's number. Seeing that it was Maggie, she said, "Please don't answer it." Taking the phone away from her, Eddie said, "I can't ignore her. She's in a very bad place right now." After he hit the talk button Robin could tell Maggie was sobbing on the other end of the line. At first she felt guilty for asking Eddie to not answer the phone, but as the conversation continued she became angry. Eddie listened to Maggie for about ten minutes and then said, "Just relax, Maggie, it'll be okay. I know this is a tough time for you, but I'm going with Robin to pick up our new puppy." Robin heard more tears and could tell this wasn't what Maggie wanted to hear. Eddie continued to listen, then suddenly he turned the car around and started to drive back to the townhouse. Robin was stunned!

Once back at the house, Eddie hung up the phone and said, "I'm really sorry, but Maggie needs me. She has no one, and today she's just in a really bad spot. I need to go pick her up, calm her down, take her for coffee, and get her out of that house for a while." Speechless, Robin couldn't believe what she was hearing. They had spent hours puppy-proofing their home and reading books on how to raise their new baby retriever. Now it wasn't going to happen because Maggie was having one of her famous meltdowns. Eddie was going to throw the day away, disappoint Robin, and leave her with the task of rescheduling a pickup time with the breeder. The breeder had already reworked her schedule to accommodate them. She'd said if they didn't pick up their puppy today she'd be obligated to sell him to another family. Eddie was risking their ability to bring their new retriever home because Maggie needed a shoulder to cry on. And, once again, it had to be his shoulder.

Feeling hurt and let down, Robin finally asked, "What about us? What about our plans for our first puppy? We've waited so long for this. Why does she always have to call you? Why can't she call her father, mother, sister, brother, minister, or a therapist?" Eddie pulled into the driveway, got out of the car. and opened the door for Robin. As she got out he replied, "Can't you be more understanding? What am I supposed to do? Maggie is our friend and she needs us right now." Robin could tell he was getting angry with her. Grabbing her purse, she asked, "If she needs us so badly, why is it that she never calls me?"

Looking at her with exasperation, Eddie handed her the pet carrier from the back seat and said, "Maggie believes I'm the only person she can talk to. My hands are tied, and I don't have a choice. She needs me and I need for you to be more considerate and understanding of the position I'm in!" Tucking her purse under one arm and a bag of doggie treats under the other, Robin took the pet carrier and replied, "And I don't need you? I don't need your support? I don't need your help? I'm not supposed to feel disappointed and upset that we may lose our puppy?" As she turned to make her way up the stairs, she tripped and dropped the pet carrier. Picking it up, she heard Eddie say from the curb, "Robin, try to be more sympathetic. Don't be so selfish. I was really looking forward to getting our dog today too. You aren't the only one who's disappointed." Robin kept on walking and didn't look back as Eddie drove away. Once inside, Robin dropped the pet carrier, threw her purse and the doggie treats onto the couch, and then broke down in tears.

By the time Eddie returned home, Robin had made arrangements to pick up the puppy the next day. She did some creative storytelling about a sick aunt in the hospital, and the breeder had finally agreed she and Eddie could still have the retriever. After taking a bath and drowning her disappointment in a big bowl of chocolate ice cream, Robin felt she'd pulled herself together enough to put her hurt behind her. When she heard Eddie coming up the stairs, she put on her best face and decided to not tell him how upset she'd felt earlier that day. Turning on the television, she saw that a rerun of Princess Diana discussing her divorce from Prince Charles was airing. As she took a seat on the couch, she thought to herself, *It could be so much worse. Eddie could be sleeping with Maggie.*

Eddie walked in with Chinese food in hand. After kissing Robin on the cheek, he went to the kitchen to serve up dinner. As she listened to Diana tell the reporter about the three people in her relationship—herself, Charles and his mistress Carmella—Robin became annoyed and said to herself, *There are three people in my relationship and that third person is named Maggie!* Eddie brought her a plate and sat down next to her on the couch. Taking a mouthful of noodles, he nodded toward the television and said, "What a royal mess that was." As they ate their dinner, Robin waited for Eddie to tell her what was happening with Maggie, but he never did.

While she was scraping the plates, putting away the leftover egg rolls and fried rice, Maggie said to Eddie, "I made arrangements to pick up our puppy tomorrow. I'm so excited I can hardly stand it!" After hanging up the dishtowel, she rejoined Eddie on the couch. He was sitting silently, looking straight at the television. Giving him a playful hug and kiss, she asked, "Did you hear me?" Eddie got up from the couch, went to the refrigerator, and took out a soda. Again, Robin said, "We can go get our puppy tomorrow. It took some smooth talking, but I convinced the breeder we would absolutely, positively be at her place tomorrow." Eddie still wouldn't answer her. "What's wrong with you? Why aren't you talking to me?" she asked. With this, Eddie put the soda down on the counter, crossed his arms across his chest and said, "We can't go tomorrow. I promised Maggie I'd help her move out of the house and into a more affordable apartment."

Robin didn't know what to do or say. Sitting on the couch, she silently watched the interview with Diana. Eddie came over to her, gave her a kiss on the cheek, and said, "Next week we can go get the puppy." Looking over at the television, he added, "I could never cheat on you. Not ever." With this he went back to the kitchen, made himself a cup of herbal tea, and said, "I'm beat. I ended up moving furniture at Maggie's. I'm going to bed." Robin remained perfectly still as Eddie made his way to the bedroom.

Once he closed the door, Robin's mind began to whirl. *What was all that about? What did he mean, he'd never cheat on me? Is there some hidden message there? And why is he so tired?* Looking at the clock, she saw that it was only eight thirty. Eddie typically stayed up till eleven. *Why is Eddie so worn out? Was he only moving furniture?* The puppy was no longer a concern as questions flew at Robin one after another. Finally she asked herself, *Is Eddie having sex with Maggie?*

Spying his cell phone on the coffee table, she picked it up and checked his text messages. What she learned shocked her. Maggie had been texting him at least ten times a day, and he'd been answering her. Checking each message, she discovered they'd made lunch dates and had met for coffee more often than she'd been aware of. Robin also noticed some back-and-forth messaging between the two—as if they were flirting teenagers. Messages like *You're such a good-looking guy* and *I bet you were super popular in high school* made Robin's skin crawl.

After looking through the text messages, Robin decided to check Eddie's e-mail. Booting up the computer, she noticed she was feeling numb and sick to her stomach. *Why didn't he tell me about all the lunch and coffee dates? Why would he be so dishonest, telling me he was busy, leaving me alone to eat so many meals by myself? How come he didn't invite me to join them?*

After clicking on Eddie's e-mail account she began looking at his inbox. Just for today, there were five messages from Maggie. She was fearful of opening them—Eddie would know she'd been snooping—so she checked his "deleted" folder instead. Again, she felt ill. There were at least thirty or forty messages from Maggie. As she looked through them she read, *No one is as good to me as you are . . . I wish Bob treated me as well as you do . . . How about drinks at my house? . . . What would I do without you? . . . You are my knight in shining armor . . . I could really fall for a guy like you . . . Robin doesn't appreciate you . . . I know I shouldn't have kissed you last night but I'm glad I did.* After reading the last e-mail, Robin picked up a large vase sitting by the computer and threw it as hard as she could against the wall. On the other side of the wall was the bedroom she shared with Eddie.

Robin needed to confront Eddie but didn't know how to go about doing so. For several weeks she'd been role-playing with me during individual sessions by reading a letter she'd written to Eddie, but hadn't given to him. Finally, during couples therapy, Robin said what she needed to say, and Eddie was coming unglued. She admitted to reading his text messages and e-mails and was now sitting on the couch glaring at Eddie, waiting for an answer she could believe. Instead Robin heard, "You're nuts! I'm not sleeping with Maggie and never have." Looking very upset and hurt, Eddie added, "You have an overactive imagination! It's just awful that you would even suggest such a thing! I've always been faithful to you! I don't cheat on you, go to strip clubs, or visit prostitutes. I'm offended you would even suspect me of sleeping around."

Robin was sitting rigidly on one end of the sofa while Eddie was angrily parked at the other end. After his tirade, they wouldn't look at one another. It was now time for Michael and me to get to work. Glancing at him, I gave him a wink. He would be taking the lead. Turning to the couple, he first spoke to Robin. "I've been working individually with Eddie for some time now, and I can honestly say I don't believe he's been unfaithful to you." Robin looked relieved but confused. Next Michael looked at Eddie and said, "No, I don't think you're sleeping with Maggie, but I do believe you're involved with her." Eddie appeared first offended and then frightened. Sitting back in his chair, Michael then announced, "It's time to start talking about emotional affairs." With this, Robin and Eddie finally looked at each other.

The Emotional Affair: Cheating without the Sex

Supportive friendships can evolve into what's known as an emotional affair. In this kind of affair, we feel emotionally empowered by a person outside of our primary relationship. We feel emotionally needed; we get emotional attention, stroking, and regular flattery. The behavior is allowed to continue, and both parties experience intoxicating mood alterations. The key point is that an emotional affair doesn't include sex itself. Although a sexual affair can start out as an emotional affair, that is not a typical sequence.

I first coined the term "emotional affair" over a quarter of a century ago, and since then many relationship experts have put their own spin on it. Though the general public has been slow to grasp the concept, the media recently became very interested in this intimacy disorder. Not long ago, a married pop music icon was accused of having an "affair of the heart" with a legendary baseball player (married). Night after night, tabloid television news shows tried to explain this high-profile "celebrity love affair without sex" to their viewing audiences, but the public didn't buy it. During this same time even my patients expressed confusion as to why a friendship would break up a marriage if sex wasn't involved. Because the emotional affair continues to be difficult to understand, I'm going to share how the idea originated and then describe why this intimacy disorder can be so destructive.

How It Can Happen: Our Story

When Michael and I first set up housekeeping together, we knew very little about how to apply mutual respect, loving boundaries, healthy intimacy, or "fair fighting" in our relationship. After a honeymoon period of about six months, we started to have a few rough moments. This is normal for any relationship, but like many couples, we weren't prepared for these bumps in the conjugal road. We rarely resolved our disagreements because we didn't know how to work through them and then let them go. Instead, both of us thought resolution was about winning the argument. Winning meant forcing the other person to accept what we individually believed was right. When this didn't work, sulking in angry, martyred silence was always the next tactic.

"Being right" at any cost is never the solution. The illusion of winning an argument or disagreement only leads to long lists of hidden resentments. Unspoken rage just stuffs relationship problems under the rug—or even the bed—and sex doesn't fix this for long. As old hurts, misunderstandings, irritations, annoyances, and aggravations build, it can start to get crowded not only under the bed but in the bed. Unresolved resentments take up a lot of space, and in many cases, healthy, connected sex gets kicked out of the bed altogether.

Michael and I couldn't resolve our relationship issues because both of us suffered from serious intimacy disorders. We didn't know how to honestly talk with one another. Neither of us had ever learned how to do this. Dysfunction attracts dysfunction. With my history, it made perfect sense for me to hook up with Michael, who came to our relationship as tool-less as I was. Ours was a match built upon stuffed emotion, secretiveness, loss, tragic trauma, hidden resentment and, eventually, a great deal of pain. We both had addiction issues and I was an active alcoholic, all of which added to the explosive mix.

After watching the infidelity in my family, I swore to myself that sex outside my primary partnership would never happen. I was going to make my relationship work. Michael was a "one woman at a time" sort of guy, so extramarital affairs weren't of interest to him either. Both of us were committed to not repeating our parents' mistakes, but as young graduate students in clinical psychology, neither of us knew how seductive and empowering an emotional affair could be. Psychology books and classrooms didn't prepare us for the devastation such an affair could inflict upon a relationship.

At that time, the emotional affair hadn't been identified or defined in psychology or psychiatry. During my mother's day, a married woman who needed a lot of male attention was called a tease or worse, while a man was seen as "friendly" or "popular with the ladies." When a woman had a close male friend outside of her primary relationship, tongues wagged and gossip would begin. If a married man was spending a lot of time with a woman in need of help or support and he wasn't having sex with her, he was seen as a nice guy who just had a gift for knowing how to talk to women. These were the myths Michael and I grew up with.

Because both of us were dedicated to becoming top-notch mental health care providers, we believed we would create a personal and professional partnership that would stand the test of time. But as the years passed, we encountered a few unforeseen glitches. When Michael didn't feel appreciated by me, or if he was disgusted by my alcoholism and prescription pill popping, he could easily find women at the office who'd tell him how wonderful he was. If I felt lonely, with Michael putting in seventy- to eighty-hour workweeks, all I had to do was begin accepting lunch invitations from men "friends" who were looking for a fling. I didn't have to have sex with them, but I sure could soak up their attentions. They listened to my problems, told me how beautiful I was, and reminded me over and over again that they'd be more than willing to step into Michael's shoes.

After five years of marriage, the resentments in our relationship began to creep out from under the bed, and we were having a hard time shoving them back into the dark corners of our lives. Eventually, we were like two roommates just trying to coexist. Michael and I were clueless about our unresolved intimacy issues as a couple. By turning to emotional affairs, each of us had our emotional needs taken care of outside of our primary relationship—and we made no effort to turn to one another and work on connecting with each other.

Our extramarital emotional affairs were as potent as hardcore drugs, but neither of us thought we were doing anything wrong because we weren't being sexually unfaithful. Healing came for me after I sobered up. Recovering women friends of mine confronted me about seeking male attention to feel better about myself. I learned I needed to start parenting those parts of me that had been so damaged. I also had to start addressing my own neediness. Surrounded by my new female mentors, I learned I'd never received healthy mothering and that I didn't have a clue about how to respect myself as a woman. During my youth my mother had been involved in many emotional and physical affairs and was never at peace with herself as a female. She died an early death and was never able to teach me how to love myself. By taking responsibility for my addictions and through healing from years of loss, I grew out of my craving for excessive flirtatious male attention. I discovered I could fill myself up with good feelings about who I was. Though this restorative time was life-altering for me, there was also a difficult side. I could now see right through my partner's behavior.

THE TIPPING POINT: MICHAEL'S EMOTIONAL AFFAIR

Michael didn't see the addictive quality of emotional affairs as quickly as I did. Though he was pleased I was healing and working on myself, he continued to surround himself with very needy women who constantly demanded his help and regularly told him he was a good listener. He didn't stop rescuing females who persistently empowered him: in fact, he was addicted to the need to be needed by women. Emotional affairs had filled up the inner emptiness both of us had felt during the first years of our marriage, but for him they were also outlets for his survival skills from childhood.

He grew up in a family where the females didn't meet the needs of little boys. Instead, he'd learned that it was his job to emotionally take care of the women in his family. When Michael was abused outside of the family, it wasn't safe for him to go to his mother for nurturing: she herself was fragile and needy, having survived the loss of her own mother to the gas chambers of the Nazi holocaust. As a young boy he knew that telling his mother about his abuse would be too much for her to handle. Because of this dynamic, Michael's emotional needs were never completely met. Sadly, he only felt as though he mattered when he was "needed" by needy women like his mother.

Now, back to our early married life. One afternoon a woman who was very demanding of Michael's attentions telephoned our house looking for him. She was married to a prescription drug addict who had a terrible gambling problem. Every time she was unhappy, she'd pick up the phone and unload on Michael about her plight in life. As I watched him talk with her I noticed the immediate mood change. He felt needed, useful, and important. Her dependence on him was filling him up: he felt as though he mattered. After hanging up he turned to me and said, "Her husband is so unavailable. If it weren't for me, I don't know who she'd turn to."

This woman would rarely talk to me, and if I happened to pick up the phone her responses were often short and even a bit frosty. These encounters always left me feeling as though I was the other woman in my husband's life. Eventually, I discovered she'd been waiting for Michael to divorce me because of my drinking, and she was upset when I sobered up! Michael had played the role of surrogate emotional spouse with her for so long that she'd assumed they'd eventually walk off arm in arm into the sunset.

Michael never had sex with her, but for me it still felt like he was cheating. I felt hurt, crazy, angry, distressed, betrayed, and sad that so much of his attention was going her way. In time I finally told Michael, "While I was drinking you had a strange sort of affair with her, and I know it's still going on." At first he was very defensive and told me he'd been faithful. But when I clarified by asking, "Did you discuss our problems with her?" he replied, "Yes." I then asked, "Why didn't you talk to another man about our difficulties? Why has it always been women?" With this he turned the tables and said, "Oh, and you never talked to other men about how you felt about me?"

After several moments and a few tears, Michael admitted, "That was a low blow. I'm sorry." But I wasn't innocent, and he did have a point. We were both guilty. Instead of talking about our issues with each other, we'd sought out relationships with people who'd empower us, feel sorry for us, and continually tell us how incredible we were. Michael and I had been emotionally cheating on each other to avoid honestly confronting the intimacy problems in our relationship. Initially, "emotionally cheating" was the only term we could think of to adequately describe the damage we had inflicted upon one another and our relationship. Though neither of us had acted out sexually, each of us had engaged in behavior that included all other aspects of an affair outside a primary relationship— and it almost destroyed our partnership.

Today, Michael and I are in recovery from all of our addictions, and we're equally responsible for the health of our relationship. As a result of our healing, we have evolved into two whole people who are responsible to one another, but not for one another. I can't expect his world to revolve around me, and he can't focus on me to distract himself from his own healing work. We had to learn that it's all right to have differing opinions, and to this day we don't always agree with one another. What's important is that we do respect each other. Over thirty years later, our relationship is stronger than ever. Michael and I have tools that enable us to maintain honest intimacy, along with skills and rules for disagreeing fairly. We will examine a number of these in chapter 11.

The Dynamics behind an Emotional Affair

Emotional affairs involve everything found in a physical affair except for the act of sex. Even though sex is lacking, these emotionally close, yet often superficial, relationships can be as damaging to a primary relationship as a full-blown sexual affair.

What sets the stage for an emotional affair? Here are some typical circumstances:

- The partners' emotional needs are not met or addressed in the relationship.
- Resentments aren't aired, discussed, and resolved.
- Untreated alcohol, drug, work, or food addictions are ignored.
- Long-term illness is not grieved or discussed.
- Rage or other emotions are used to manipulate.
- Children are used as buffers.
- The couple has a sense of emptiness or a lack of connection.
- A past sexual affair hasn't been fully resolved (even if it's a secret), an intimacy phobia is present, or a sexual addiction hasn't been treated.
- Sexual concerns, difficulties, or issues are ignored and never talked about.

- Emotions aren't addressed when stressors occur such as a death in the family, extended family issues, financial problems, job change or relocation, unaddressed aging issues, difficulty with children, or other major life events.

In contrast to one common pattern with physical affairs, there usually isn't a conscious decision to go looking for a an extramarital partner for cheating purposes. There may not even be sexual attraction for an emotional affair to develop. In spite of this, for a significant other it can feel just like a physical affair is occurring.

A person whose partner is having an emotional affair may tend to:

- sense distancing behavior from the partner and not know why
- suspect secretiveness, dishonesty, or half-truths from the partner
- notice unexplained credit card charges or monies spent
- notice the partner is spending more time away from home
- feel unconnected during sex
- feel unattractive, overweight, old, and undesirable to the partner
- act out with food addictions
- notice unusual telephone calls, letters, e-mails, or text messages
- feel jealous of the partner's associations with members of the opposite sex, or same sex if gay or lesbian
- feel a need to spy on a partner, not trusting what the partner says
- feel crazy, self-destructive, stupid, depressed, rageful, or even suicidal

Recovering from an Emotional Affair

When a couple comes to our office for marital counseling, Michael and I usually see them together for a number of sessions. Then I'll typically see the woman in individual therapy and Michael will work with the man. If the couple is gay, lesbian, or transgender, we'll meet several times as a group before determining who will work with whom individually. We discovered some time back that a couple working together with just one therapist was in an awkward situation because one partner usually felt like the odd person out. Doing therapy with couples as a couple has been very therapeutic for those we've had the pleasure of assisting. About one-third of our relationship practice involves couples suffering from the consequences of emotional affairs.

There really aren't any quick relationship fixes, nothing etched in stone. Each person, couple, and situation is unique. But couples can heal from emotional affairs, and we've discovered some guidelines that we encourage couples and individuals to follow. Although they apply to all relationships, when a couple is recovering from an emotional affair they are absolutely essential.

- It's all right to disagree, but respect is a must.

- Learn how to fight fairly (see the appendix for books on fair fighting).

- Personal space is a must. Asking for time away from the relationship is perfectly normal. Having same-sex safe friends balances us out emotionally.

- Go to bed angry if you have to. Taking a break in the heat of an argument provides a cooling-off period. Once the emotions have died down, rational conversation can begin again.

- We don't have to always like or approve of our mate's behavior or actions. Respectfully sharing how we feel keeps resentments out from under the bed.

- Having separate territories is essential. Boundaries around personal property and territory keeps relationships from becoming enmeshed and it shouts, "I respect my partner's need for privacy!" My closet looks like a bomb hit it. Once Michael tried to organize it, and I couldn't find a thing! And he doesn't like it when I eat food off his plate without asking.

- Talk about sex, and ask questions. Too many couples avoid discussing sex. One person will believe all is well in the bedroom while the other is feeling miserable, dissatisfied, or uncomfortable. Talking about sex and having sexual boundaries improves intimacy between couples.

- We don't have to totally embrace our partner's family and friends unless we want to. For example, during a couples therapy session a man said to his fiancée, "You're marrying me, not my family, so stop worrying."

- Have hobbies and interests outside the relationship. Michael loves golf. I'm a beach fan. Having different interests and activities makes us more fascinating, well-rounded, whole people. This in turn enriches our relationship.

- If you find yourself spending more time with members of the opposite sex (same sex for gays and lesbians) than you are with your partner, ask yourself, "Am I talking about my partner with people who aren't interested in the stability and health of my relationship?"

- Watch out for potential emotional affairs during rough times in the relationship. Talk it out with your partner or a licensed therapist.

- Finally, have fun as a couple. Make time for the relationship. Try new things together and take at least an hour a day to catch up with each other.

Although the emotional affair is the most common difficulty found between couples, a host of other stumbling blocks can trip up a relationship. In the remaining pages of this book you'll read about other obsessive and addictive behaviors that are common roadblocks to intimacy. I suggest you examine each of the following chapters closely. Even if you think the chapter titles don't apply to your situation, you just might come across that one paragraph that will provide you with the solution you are looking for.

• • •

5

Why We Can't See the Dancing Elephant: The Alcoholic, the Addict, and the Co-addict

*A few years back I was more a candidate for skid row bum
than an Emmy. If I hadn't stopped [drinking],
I'd be playing handball with John Belushi right now.*

— JOHN LARROQUETTE, ACTOR, COMEDIAN, AND RECOVERING ALCOHOLIC

Michael and I were watching a Mardi Gras parade in our town when we noticed two of our clients standing directly across the street from us. They were easy to spot, as they were arguing fiercely with one another.

Andy and Jordan initially came to see us for marital therapy. Andy had had an affair but wanted to repair his relationship with his wife. The couple had been married for close to ten years, and both parents were very devoted to their three young daughters. Jordan worked as a secretary for a physician, and Andy was an electrician. Michael and I met with them as a couple and asked them to bring into therapy a list of what they considered to be difficulties in the marriage.

Jordan was furious about Andy's affair, but she had a hard time expressing it productively. Tall and trim, with shoulder-length brown hair, she sat on the couch in tears, looking like a wounded little girl. After a few tears, Jordan said, "I can't believe he actually screwed her! She was part of our social circle, and she always acted as if I were her favorite person!" Jordan's pain emanated from every part of her body. Andy, who in middle age was still a handsome man, tried to reach over and comfort his wife, but she briskly brushed his hand away.

Andy had decided his affair was not something he wanted to continue, and he had told his wife about it. "I know what I did was wrong and I'll do anything to make it up," he said. This only made Jordan even more upset. Without saying a word she picked a pillow up off the couch and smacked him across the face. Getting up and taking the pillow from Jordan, I said, "No physical violence. If this continues, Michael and I will not be able to work with either of you. Jordan, I know you are angry and I'll be glad to do anger work with you during an individual session." With this Jordan began to sob uncontrollably.

To work on his shame about the affair, Andy began seeing Michael for individual therapy. During their sessions he also expressed concern about Jordan's drinking. I worked with Jordan individually, and as the therapy continued, she expressed her rage over her husband's infidelity. But as time went on I noticed she wasn't getting any relief. One afternoon I said, "I remember you telling me you were on an antidepressant, but when I asked you about other medications you never answered me. Aside from the antidepressant, what medications are you taking?" Looking surprised, she replied, "Well, I told you I was taking a hydrocodone drug for pain." I had suspected this, but she had never admitted to me she was using this strong, dangerously addictive medication.

Hydrocodone is a semi-synthetic opioid derived from naturally occurring opiates. An opioid or opiate is a chemical substance that numbs pain in the body. (Heroin is also a semi-synthetic opiod.) In the United States hydrocodone is given in combination with acetaminophen, aspirin, ibuprofen, or certain antihistamines (to relieve its itching side effects). Pain medications containing hydrocodone are marketed under such brand names as Vicodin, OxyContin, Percocet, Demerol, and Darvon. Though it is a useful pain medication, it can also be extremely addictive, and in recent years, alarm about the abuse of prescription painkillers has risen dramatically.

In reviewing Jordan's use of a hydrocodone-based medication, I discovered she was not taking the drug as prescribed but illegally ordering it from Internet sites and consuming nearly lethal doses. She also added she drank wine nightly and took antihistamines.

Looking at her, I thought back to the days when I too abused medications prescribed to me for Crohn's disease. I had chased very strong pain pills with beer, so I understood just how dangerous Jordan's situation was. She was going to need medical assistance to detox off the pills and alcohol. "I can't work with you as long as you are addictively consuming drugs and alcohol," I told her. "As I say to all patients in your position, it's a waste of your money and my time to continue with outpatient therapy. How do you feel about going into treatment for chemical dependency at an inpatient facility?" At this question, Jordan began to cry again. Watching her absorb the seriousness of her situation, I could see that she was also relieved. After she dried her eyes, she looked at me and said, "I've always known I needed to do something about this." She entered a treatment facility the very next day.

Jordan successfully completed treatment, and she and Andy returned to couples therapy six months later. Sitting on the couch, they seemed irritable and uncomfortable. "Sex is awful," Jordan announced. "And he's always mad at me because I go to so many Alcoholics Anonymous and Narcotics Anonymous meetings. Now that I've quit drinking and taking pills, he nags at me nonstop about the cigarettes. I've been sober for six months, and I'm smoking a lighter brand of cigarettes, but I'm not ready to give them up completely." Looking at Andy, I said, "It sounds to me like Jordan is making great progress."

Then Michael asked Andy, "Are you going to the support group for family members of alcoholics and addicts called Al-Anon?" With irritation he replied, "No. I'm not going to waste my time sitting in a room listening to a bunch of strangers whine. This is her problem. She's the one who drank and took pills and wouldn't have sex with me. I've realized I had to go out and have an affair." Again, Jordan grabbed a pillow and whacked Andy on the side of the head. This time Michael took the pillow away from Jordan, and again I found myself saying to her, "Jordan, you know the rules. No hitting or physical violence. It you are angry, just say so."

Obviously upset, Jordan replied, "I did not make him have an affair, and I'm angry he is blaming me for this. He decided to call this woman up and arranged to meet her at a motel. Yes I'm a drunk and an addict, but I'm not going to take responsibility for his cheating. If he was so unhappy with me, he could have divorced me!" Turning to Michael in shock, Andy asked, "She's not going to acknowledge that her alcoholism and drug addiction killed our sex life and ruined our marriage? She's going to ignore how her behavior, her drunk behavior, scared our kids? She's not going to take responsibility for all of the worry she caused me, my parents, and her parents? What do you think, doc? If you had been in my situation wouldn't you have found another woman to give you the attention you needed?"

With anger seeping out of every pore of her being, Jordan said, "As for sex, we have never had a great sex life. Our sex life has been all about satisfying you. You have never asked me how I feel about sex or what I need sexually. Do you ever consider that I'm a sexual abuse survivor and that there are certain acts of sex, acts you insist upon, that turn me off?" Surprised, Andy shook his head no.

"And as for our parents," Jordan continued, "your mother takes a handful of pills every day and your father hasn't drawn a sober breath after eight PM for as long as I've been married to you!" Again, Andy looked shocked. Turning to me, Jordan began to tear up again. "I just hate how my addictions have hurt my kids. Just hate it." Then turning angrily back to Andy, she said, "But who nominated you father of the year? When was the last time you were home from work before seven to have dinner with the children? You've missed school plays, dance recitals, family gatherings, and even my birthday. My best friend threw a birthday party for me and you arrived late! On my birthday!" Sitting back into the couch, Jordan angrily crossed her arms.

Looking at both Andy and Jordan, I asked, "Have either of you ever honestly shared with each other what it is you don't like about one another?" Both of them shook their head no. Michael then asked, "Do you guys ever talk about sex? What you like or don't like about sex? How you feel when you are sexual with each other?" Again, both of them shook their heads no. With this I added, "And what about problems with family or in-laws? Do you two ever take the time to sit down and discuss problems with relatives?" In unison both Andy and Jordan said, "no." Turning to Jordan I asked, "Were you ever honest with Andy about your feelings when he was late for your birthday or missed family get-togethers or dance recitals?" Jordan looked at Andy and then at me and said, "Well, he should know! Why do I have to tell him! Just like he should know sex with him isn't always wonderful!" Again surprised, Andy asked, "How am I supposed to know you aren't enjoying our sex life if you don't say anything? That the incest was still so painful for you?"

Finally Michael said, "It's important for both of you to know that resolving old conflict in a relationship is essential. Clearing away resentment will promote healthy intimacy. As long as Jordan was blunting her emotions with drugs and alcohol, she was never going to be able to work through any of her relationship issues with you, Andy. She needs those meetings. And no, Jordan, you are not responsible for his affair, or his compulsive work addiction, but you can't expect him to know when you are upset if you don't say anything." Turning to Andy, I added, "It's not fair of you to blame her for your decisions. She didn't force you to have an affair or to work compulsively. You have addictions in need of your attention and recovery."

Looking at both of them I said, "Each of you is 50 percent responsible for the damage, resentment, dysfunction, and illness in this relationship. You can divorce one another, not look at your own behavior, continue to blame your partner for everything, and then get into another relationship as sick as this one is—or you can make a decision to heal individually and as a couple. Healing means taking responsibility for your addictions and behavior, learning how to have healthy boundaries, fight fairly, and be involved in your own individual healing process with support groups and if need be, more therapy."

That day Jordan and Andy did decide to work on the relationship and begin the process of healing as a couple. Several months later there they were, standing across the street from Michael and me, arguing with one another. As the Mardi Gras floats began their slow, colorful procession down the street, Michael and I also noticed Jordan and Andy were holding hands. Chuckling, I said to Michael, "I think they're going to be okay!"

Addiction: The Relationship Annihilator

The disease of chemical dependency—the addiction to alcohol, prescription drugs, or illegal substances—directly impacts one out of every three families in the United States. Active addiction involves the compulsive use of a mood-altering substance in spite of personal, social, health, job-related, physical, legal, or financial consequences. Some of us picture alcoholics and addicts as scruffy characters without jobs or families, living under an overpass and eating out of tin cans. In actuality, people from every walk of life can suffer from this emotionally devastating, physiologically destructive disease: lawyers, students, doctors, schoolteachers, you name it. I've seen twelve-year-old chemically dependent clients as well as seniors in their eighties.

Before an addict or alcoholic in a relationship can recognize how addiction hurts a relationship—much less create a healthy intimate one—the topic of sobriety must first be tackled. And the other person in the relationship, known as the co-addict, needs to take responsibility to change his or her own enabling, controlling, or caretaking behavior. Trying to work through difficult relationship issues when addiction and co-addiction are present is a waste of time. We can't clean up the other problems—money, sex, intimacy, communication, family, employment, physical, emotional, and spiritual—if we ignore addiction and co-addiction.

Good Help Is Hard to Find

Patients come to my office and tell me that their last helping professional just didn't seem to understand their problems. The solutions they got were short-lived at best. Many of these patients knew there was a problem but couldn't identify it. Some only suspected addiction, and others were unaware that it was a problem. Even the more aware patients sometimes have trouble getting help: for instance, people who keep attracting partners with substance abuse problems and want to change the pattern, or couples who know they have substance abuse problem but don't know what to do about it.

If addiction is so prevalent in our society, why does the system fail addicts and their families time after time? When someone is upset about a partner's substance use, often the first person they share their worry with is their family physician, who typically has received very little training on addiction in medical school. The professional who is uneducated about addiction can actually create more difficulties for a couple struggling with chemical dependency. How often I have heard comments like these: "I was concerned about my husband's drinking, so I talked to my family doctor. He suggested I tell my husband to cut back," and "My wife was drinking more and more at night, so my psychologist told me to start measuring out her liquor for her." Cutting down on chemical intake will not resolve a substance addiction. Being abstinent and adopting new behaviors are essential.

What about mental health professionals? The general public tends to believe most psychologists, social workers, psychiatrists, therapists, and counselors have an understanding of chemical dependency. This is a myth. Mental health professionals constantly misdiagnose addiction as bipolar disorder, borderline personality, antisocial behavior, depression, phobic reactions, or anxiety. In extreme cases, addicts are even diagnosed as being schizophrenic or psychotic.

Why does this happen? Mental health care providers are people with problems just like you and me. They may

- have substance abuse problems themselves

- be in a relationship with an active alcoholic or addict

- have children who are chemically dependent

- suffer from untreated issues related to being raised as children in homes where one or both parents were addicted to alcohol, illegal drugs, or prescription medication

Sigmund Freud, the father of modern psychology and a notorious cocaine addict, believed his profession attracted people who had suffered. I agree with him, and I also know that many of my peers have not healed from their suffering. Among all of the medical specialties, students going into psychiatry are reported to have the highest incidents of substance abuse. A survey given to counseling psychologists about substance abuse in the profession had some interesting results, reported by Good and colleagues in a 1995 article in *Counseling Psychologist*. The study found that 43 percent of the respondents reported knowing a male psychologist with a drinking problem, and 28 percent said they knew a female colleague with a drinking problem.

In extreme cases, therapists have advised couples to divorce or separate—while still failing to help them address issues of chemical dependency. No matter how dysfunctional a relationship is, it's rarely my job to counsel a couple to divorce or separate. It's also not my place to tell patients who they can or can't date. Any helping professional who believes otherwise is overstepping a boundary. And this is especially true when chemical dependency is involved.

Two in One

Some helping professionals may have difficulty focusing on the disease of chemical dependency because they don't know how to distinguish "addict" behavior from "nonaddict" behavior. If we are the partner of an addict, we most likely have the same problem. The following test may help you understand why professionals and partners have a hard time putting a finger on addiction. If you are now in a relationship with an active addict or alcoholic, or have a history of attracting substance abusers as partners, try this experiment. (Have some paper and a pen or pencil available to do the writing part of the exercise.)

Close your eyes and visualize your current or most recent partner. Next, think back and visualize this person during the first few months or even years of your relationship. Look closely. What is it that attracted you? Open your eyes and list five things about this partner that originally attracted you.

Now close your eyes again. Remember a time when your partner was intoxicated. Notice the difference from the person you fell in love with. List five things you really dislike about this intoxicated person.

Finally, close your eyes again. Visualize the person you originally fell in love with standing next to the intoxicated alcoholic or addict. First, look at the person you fell in love with and imagine saying, "I miss you." See what happens. Next, look at the addict or alcoholic and say, "I'm angry with you. You are keeping me from this person I love." Once you are able to separate the addict personality from the person you fell in love with, take a moment to write out these differences.

In the future, when you see your loved one reacting with addict behavior, remind yourself that you're not dealing with the person you fell in love with. So you may need to lower your expectations and understand that addicts and alcoholics, in their addiction, do not always think, act, or behave appropriately, especially if they are under the influence of a mood-altering chemical. Such a person can be under the influence and those around them will be completely unaware of it. And even when not under the influence, the person is still controlled by the disease of chemical dependency and its impacts on thinking patterns.

Here is your dilemma, and it's one most mental health professionals don't understand. The addict or alcoholic you currently love or have loved in the past still resides behind the walls of addiction, even when not intoxicated. When you catch a glimpse of this person, you believe change is happening. Many mental health professions react the same way. When they catch a glimpse of the person you love—sober, articulate, and remorseful—they too have hope, believing psychiatric medications and talk therapies are creating a cure. But if there has not been adequate intervention on the addiction, other issues, such as personal boundaries, sexuality, infidelity, resentments, communication patterns, parenting, and finances, can't be addressed in a healthy, healing manner. Once therapy ends, relationship difficulties once thought resolved will resurface.

For this reason, it is essential that you view your partner as two separate people: the person you fell in love with and the addict who is keeping you from the one you love. When you do this, you can then take steps to protect yourself when you see that your partner is under the influence of a mood-altering substance, or in "addictive thinking" even when not intoxicated. Recognizing when your partner is in the disease's grip will help you understand that rational discussion and communication will not happen, and that your expectations will most likely not be met. I often advise co-addicts never to argue with a partner when the disease of chemical dependency has taken over. Instead, I suggest calling a friend for support, visiting a relative, taking a walk around the block, writing about the incident, or soaking in a bubble bath.

Speaking of co-addiction, let's take a closer look at this role and what it means.

What Is Co-addiction?

If we aren't able to see the addict versus the person we love, we are mostly likely a co-addict. Co-addicts typically react to addiction in several key ways.

1. They will enable the chemically dependent partner by making excuses for unacceptable behavior, failing to hold the loved one accountable for the negative consequences of the alcoholism or drug addiction.

2. Co-addicts often believe that if they only were shorter, taller, skinnier, younger, richer, or smarter, their love relationships wouldn't be so trouble-filled, so they work double-time to meet what they perceive as their partner's needs and wants.

3. They seek revenge for their partner's abuse of alcohol or drugs by controlling finances; they may also overspend.

4. Some co-addicts withhold sex to punish an addicted partner; they may also bad-mouth the partner, even giving children information about the addict that is not appropriate for small ears.

Chemically dependent people may be experts at coming up with excuses for their addict behavior, but co-addicts are masters. Many co-addicts have difficulty recognizing addiction in a partner with a good income. As one woman said to me, "He brings home a great paycheck every week, and he doesn't go to the bars. How can he be an alcoholic when he just sits in front of the television and drinks? I don't think he has an alcohol problem. No, he just needs to pay more attention to me."

Then there are co-addicts who believe that if their partner is physically attractive, addiction can't be a problem. One client told me, "My girlfriend is in great shape. Yes, she likes her pot and smokes it every single day, but she's not an addict. I know what drug addicts look like, and that's not her. But when she's high she does spend a lot of money online. How can I get her to quit running up the credit cards?"

My all-time favorite comment comes from a woman who said, "He is so creative! I really think the stress and the demands of his job just do him in. Yes, at night his back hurts him terribly, so I know he is using quite a bit of a narcotic pain medication. I found out he has also been using pain medication in the afternoon. I thought maybe this was causing impotency for him, but when I asked he said, 'What does this have to do with our dead sex life?' He said we don't have sex that often because he's just too tired."

Well heavens, yes! I'd be too sleepy for sex if I were taking a narcotic pain medication addictively! Wouldn't you?

Am I in a Relationship with an Addict?

When I'm visiting with a new patient, I always have concerns about addiction when I hear comments like these:

- She drinks every night to get to sleep.
- He goes to the bar every evening after work.
- She has had several DWIs.
- He lost a job because he had been drinking.
- She has lost all motivation since she started smoking pot.
- He takes pills to lose weight, and they make him really hyper, but he doesn't think it's a problem.

- The kids complain about her falling asleep on the couch in the middle of the afternoon after she takes these funny pills.

- He seems to think he has to get drunk every time he attends a barbeque or sporting event.

- She can only have sex or really tell me how she feels after doing a line of coke.

- He said he doesn't know how all those bar charges ended up on our credit card.

- When she doesn't drink she's fine, but when she picks up a drink I never know what to expect.

If you suspect or are concerned that your partner may have a substance abuse problem, turn to the chapter 5 worksheet in appendix A in the back of this book and answer each of the questions with a yes or no. When you're done, return to this page.

If you answered yes to three of more questions, your partner just might be chemically dependent. If this is the case, know that none of your relationship issues will ever be resolved until you take some action.

What Can I Do?

A therapist with a background in chemical dependency who specializes in relationships can often provide the gentle guidance needed to begin the road to recovery from addiction and, ultimately, build intimacy. We also suggest finding a treatment facility that emphasizes support groups for treating alcoholism, rather than strictly relying on medications. And find helping professionals who are recovering from the disease of chemical dependency themselves, either as addicts, alcoholics, or co-addicts. They often provide excellent health care to individuals, couples, and families impacted by addiction. In addition:

Educate yourself about the disease of chemical dependency. Go online and read up on addiction (see this book's Resources section for reliable Internet sources). Learn about alcoholism, illegal substance use, and addiction to prescription medications. Recognize that you cannot relieve your partner of an addiction. It's not your job, and it never was. You didn't cause it or create it, but you are probably allowing it to continue.

Get honest with yourself about how you are contributing to the addiction with by rationalizing, justifying, and minimizing the alcohol or chemical use. Get honest about how much your partner is drinking or using drugs.

Stop covering up for your partner. The loving response is to allow your partner the dignity of suffering the natural consequences of alcohol and drug use. Stop intervening on your partner's consequences.

Get support for yourself from groups like Al-Anon or Co-Dependents Anonymous, or visit your local drug and alcohol council. Go to an open meeting of Alcoholics Anonymous or Narcotics Anonymous to learn about addiction, see what recovering families look like, and hear that you are not alone in your struggle. Though you may think you have enough support in your life, chances are you have been isolating or don't have enough of the right kind of support.

If single, hold back on sex before you know a new partner well. When dating, know that it will take three to six months for you to recognize the symptoms of alcoholism or drug addiction in a potential partner. Jumping into the sack too soon often complicates relationships. Get to know each other first and see if you can be friends before you become lovers.

If in a relationship, don't use sex or money as a retaliatory weapon. If your partner is sober and you feel like having sex, go for it. But never have sex when your partner is intoxicated or when you don't want to. And watch that compulsive spending. Many co-addicts will spend in anger to get back at their partner. This may feel good temporarily, but in the end all you have is financial debt, which creates emotional stress.

Don't accept unacceptable treatment or behavior from a chemically dependent partner. Stop making excuses. If it feels bad, if it hurts, or if it feels wrong, trust your gut and speak up. Otherwise you are encouraging inappropriate alcohol or drug behavior and letting the addiction persist.

Have a place to go when you feel overwhelmed by the addiction. Make arrangements with parents or friends ahead of time in case you need to spend the night away from home. Leaving doesn't have to mean the relationship is over. It means you're saying, "As long as addictive behavior is going on, I'm going to take care of myself and remove myself from the situation."

If you have children, explain to them, in language they will understand, that their parent (or your partner) is addicted to drugs or alcohol. Be sure to let them know they did not cause the problem. If you need help discussing this with young children, read them the children's book *The Brown Bottle* by Penny Jones. For older children and young teenagers, try Claudia Black's book *My Dad Loves Me, My Dad Has a Disease: A Child's View— Living with Addiction.*

Check your own addictions. Many co-addicts can't see that alcohol or drug dependency is an issue in their relationships because they themselves are numbing their emotions with addictive spending, workaholic or busy-holic behavior, compulsive eating, bulimia, anorexia compulsive gambling, religious obsessions, sex addiction, alcoholism or drug abuse, codependency, or addiction to martyrdom and self-righteousness. Heal yourself.

Finally, know that you are addicted to the stress that living with chemical dependency creates whenever you're involved with an addict or an alcoholic. Every time you are confronted with the chaos addiction produces, your body begins producing large quantities of adrenaline. It's like getting zapped with a bolt of electricity over and over again. When this happens our senses sharpen, our breath rate and blood pressure rise, our muscles tighten, and the body gears up for flight or a fight. And each jolt of adrenaline counters our depression, grief, and sense of loneliness. For this reason alone, we may leave one chemically dependent relationship only to find ourselves in another one before we've even healed from the first! Because we are unable to feel our emotions, our anger turns to despair while our grief and sadness become depression. Jumping into another dysfunctional relationship gets that adrenaline pumping and temporarily "fixes" our depression.

· · ·

Take responsibility for getting well. Not only will it improve your health, but it will increase your current partner's chances for getting sober. Your recovery will also decrease your children's risk for being in future relationships like yours. If you are single, and you do the work necessary to heal yourself, you will be less at risk for attracting an active alcoholic or addict into your life in the future. Chemical dependency can be at the core of relationship problems, but sadly, this fact is often not recognized. Understanding how addiction works is the key to repairing a chemically dependent relationship. By first addressing the core issue of addiction and co-addiction, other intimacy and relationship concerns can finally find resolution and healing.

• • •

6

Work Addiction: The Socially Accepted Intimacy Buffer

*I'm a workaholic. Before long I'm traveling on my nervous energy
alone. This is incredibly exhausting.*

— EVA GABOR, COMEDIC ACTRESS, MARRIED FIVE TIMES

While finishing up a call to my husband on my cell phone, I entered my
office and saw a man sitting on the couch. Rather than waiting in the
reception room, he had apparently decided it was time for his session to
begin. As soon as I closed the phone and tucked it into my skirt pocket,
my client Lucas sarcastically said, "I don't know why I'm the only one
who's sitting on this couch." Looking around the room, he added, "There
should be two of us here." The first thing I noticed about this middle-
aged man was that his sandy blond hair kept falling over his eyes. He
nervously tried to push it back, but the gesture was useless.

Lucas was a new client. He was several minutes early for the session
and clearly agitated. Within just a few moments, I could tell that he wasn't
pleased about finding himself in a therapist's office. He sat slumped on the
leather couch, both his attitude and physical posture screaming "I don't
want to be here!" Looking up at me, he also appeared to be very angry.

Because it was just about time to start the therapy session, I went
ahead and closed the door to the office. Before I could sit down he
asked, "Why have I been singled out as the problem? And where is my
wife? She was supposed to meet me here to discuss 'my behavior' in this

marriage. I really thought this would have been important enough for her to be here on time. Guess I was wrong." Changing positions he crossed both his arms and legs and started to sulk. I could tell this session was going to be very interesting.

"Why do you think you're here?" I asked. Shaking his head, he shot back, "Let's get one thing straight! I'm not the only problem in this marriage! I agreed to come to therapy just to appease my wife, hoping maybe we could both see how we are contributing to the difficulties in our relationship." Agitated, he looked at his watch and then continued. "I feel like Betty is going to be late on purpose, because she really doesn't think any of our problems have a thing to do with her. In her eyes, everything that goes wrong or is wrong is my fault. Betty tells me I'm unappreciative, that I don't respect her, her job, and all that she does for the family. She said I was the one who needed the help."

With irritation he pulled out a pack of nicotine gum and pushed a stick of it into his mouth. "She wanted me to quit smoking, and I did. She asked me to do more around the house, and I do. She wanted me to take over more of the parenting duties, and I have! When she comes home from work and goes directly to her office to toil away some more on paperwork and telephone calls, I give her space. If she has a late work-related meeting and needs to cancel social or family functions, I do it for her. I try and I try, and nothing pleases her! To be honest with you, I'm really beginning to believe that the only time she is truly happy is when she is away from me, working."

Watching him angrily chomp on the nicotine gum, I asked, "Do you know nicotine gum is addictive and that it represses anger and fear? Usually, I ask folks not to smoke cigarettes or chew nicotine gum thirty minutes before visiting the office, but in your case, it looks like this gum just might be holding you together. How many sticks are you chewing each day?"

Looking a bit surprised Lucas replied, "No kidding? I figured it was addictive, but I didn't know the stuff buried anger. No wonder I can't quit using it. I must be pretty angry because I'm chewing a bucketload of this gum every day. And it's hitting my wallet, too." Crossing his arms more tightly, he added sarcastically, "I pay for it myself, but Betty complains about that too! Do you know she actually told me that because of her job, she can bring in more income to cover expenses like my nicotine gum? I cannot believe she really thinks this!"

Pushing his hair out of his eyes again, he continued, "I was really upset one evening because she and I were supposed to go to the movies. It had been weeks since we'd had any alone time together. But just before we were supposed to leave for the theater, she announced to me she couldn't go. Instead, she shut herself up in the office at home and worked till midnight. When I told her how disappointed I was, she gave me a lecture about the cost of my gum. And she doesn't shell out a dime for it!"

It was easy to see that Lucas felt he had been identified as the difficulty in the marriage by his wife. Looking at my office clock, I too began to wonder where Betty was. She had called my office earlier to say a work-related situation had come up and that she'd be at the session as soon as she could get away. From her message, I had initially assumed she would arrive just a few minutes late, but now the session was almost half over and only Lucas was sitting on my old leather couch. When I asked him how he felt about his wife running so late for their first marital therapy session, he pulled out another piece of gum and mockingly said, "This is nothing new. She's always late. There's always some big crisis at work that she just has to attend to. In her mind, no one else can handle it!"

While we continued to wait, Lucas told me he was a high school math teacher who also coached football. He talked briefly about the people he worked with and the kids in his classes, but then his eyes really lit up when he started describing what he loved about coaching. One of his sons was on the football team, and Lucas believed they would win the state championship.

With pride he said, "I just started coaching five years ago. Because I played college football I'm very familiar with the game. When I was first asked to take over the team I was hesitant, but when I saw the last coach I decided I had more to offer than he did. The team was initially in terrible shape, but after a lot of hard work, I've finally got a great group of players. It's been pure joy to watch these kids come together as a team."

Lucas suddenly seemed more relaxed and animated. "Having my oldest son on the team has really been a lot of fun. He doesn't want special treatment, so I have to watch myself. In a few years my youngest son will also be able to play on the team. By then his brother will have graduated, so he'll get to have his own experience." Pulling out his wallet, he asked, "Do you want to see their pictures?" After looking at the photographs of the two blond-headed brothers, I said, "What good-looking kids," then asked, "What does your wife do professionally?"

As he put the wallet back in his jacket pocket, his dark mood returned. "Betty manages a bunch of these health food stores. For someone who preaches holistic health and nutrition every chance she gets, you would think she would follow her own advice." Angrily, he continued, "If I go to visit her at the office, or stop in at one of the stores to pick up some supplements, there she is, dispensing words of wisdom to customers about good nutrition, herbal remedies, supplements, healthy living, and a balanced life. And do you know what is so ironic?" I shook my head no. "Betty is the most out-of-balance person I know! She works constantly, never takes vacations, eats poorly, gets hardly any sleep, no exercise, spends little time with the boys, let alone me, and constantly complains about how hard she works."

Lucas got up and tossed a wad of gum into the trash can. After he sat down he said, "I have a great job with incredible benefits. Betty doesn't need to work as hard as she does. If she didn't work at all we would have to tighten our belts a bit, but we would still be fine. I understand her desire to work, and when our kids were young we had agreed that when the time was right, she should pursue a job that was of interest to her. Once the boys were older, she got this job, what she calls her dream job, managing a chain of organic health food stores. Betty has always been interested in the holistic health market. As a matter of fact, we met in a funky health food store when we were both in college. For years I called her my little hippie chick because she cooked organic and was a die-hard vegetarian. The boys grew up with homemade baby foods, herbal teas, and natural health remedies. Those were fun times." I could tell Lucas was remembering better days, so for a moment we sat in silence.

After looking at his watch again, he continued. "Betty is good at this job, and I know it's both interesting and very challenging, but it's like a monster, an all-consuming monster! What's healthy about that? I have really tried to be supportive of her and her job. On my lunch break I'll try to have lunch with Betty at one of her stores, on her schedule, but she'll still be too busy to sit down and have a quick bite with me. Sometimes, I'll eat by myself and then get upset and just walk out. I swear, most of the time I don't think she even realizes I've left!"

Lucas crossed his arms across his chest. "Betty and I have no life. None! Our sex life is almost nonexistent. The boys and I eat dinner by ourselves and we save a plate for her, but when she comes home at seven, eight, nine, ten, or even eleven o'clock at night, she's too tired to eat. She's always late for football games, school functions, and this year she even missed a birthday dinner for our youngest son. He was crushed."

There was pain in Lucas's eyes as he talked at length about the impact on their boys. "When I ask her why she has to work so many hours, she tells me she's doing it for the family. I don't believe this for one second. For several years I bought into that myth, but not anymore. The truth of the matter is I feel like Betty gets more from her career than she does from me or the boys, and that's why she works so much."

Over the years I have seen many families destroyed by workaholic behavior, and obviously this family was affected too. What I also recognized was that Lucas didn't have a clue that his wife was most likely a work addict. It was apparent that he was personalizing the lack of intimacy in their relationship, not realizing that workaholism was a mood-altering condition that produces an intense stress-induced adrenaline high—a high that can be addictive. Education about workaholism would be a beginning step, but first I wanted to meet Betty.Checking the clock, I was beginning to wonder if she would ever show up. Just a few minutes were left in the allotted time.

"I just don't get it," Lucas said. "If I question Betty about her work or say anything about a missed dinner date or Sunday hike in the mountains, she tells me I'm selfish, that I need to back off, that I don't appreciate her or that I'm putting too much pressure on her. Is it me? Does she work these long hours to avoid me? She says she loves me and the boys more than anything in the world, but I don't understand. If she loves us so much, why can't she just take time to be with us?"

Suddenly the office door flew open. Standing in the doorway was a woman on a cell phone. "No, I can't accept that. We need to reorder. I'll get right on it as soon as I can. Don't worry. I'll take care of everything." After hanging up her cell phone, she happily said, "Hi! I'm Betty. I'm so very sorry I'm late. Things are just nuts at work and I couldn't get away." Turning to Lucas, she leaned over and gave him a quick peck on the cheek. "Hi, baby! How are you doing? I know, I promised to not let work make me late, but I just couldn't help it." Lucas hung his head and said nothing.

After quickly glancing around the office, Betty smiled and sat down on the couch. Taking her husband's hand she said, "Honey, I'm here. I hope you understand my situation. It was an emergency at work, and I just had to take care of it. But I'm here now." Again her cell phone began to ring. Pulling it out of her purse, she looked at it and said, "Oh, this can wait. Nothing more will disrupt our session." She was looking at me, and I could see that adrenaline was pumping through Betty's body. Her face was flushed, and she seemed glowing and energized. She was as high as a drug addict who had just ingested a mood-altering substance. Work addicts don't need to take drugs to alter mood: their body produces chemicals that are more than capable of doing it for them. After patting her distressed husband on the hand, she again turned to me and asked, "Can we get started now?"

Looking at the clock again, I saw that the session time was over. I knew my next client would be showing up any minute. Turning to Betty I said, "I'm very happy to finally meet you, but sadly our time together needs to come to an end, because the therapy hour is up." With irritation, Betty replied, "But I'm here now and you have no idea just how tough it was for me to leave my last store and drive all the way over here. Now that I've made it, you can give us a few extra minutes, can't you?"

Looking at Betty, I saw a workaholic woman who truly believed I needed to adjust my schedule to her work agenda. Obviously upset, she continued, "Just a few minutes. We have waited so long for this appointment and we both looked so forward to it. Can't you see how important this is to us? I would think that you would give us just a bit more of your time in order to hear what I have to say." Though part of her seemed to know she had crossed a line in expecting me to push my next client back to accommodate her late arrival, apparently another part of her still expected me to do so. In my experience as a clinician I had found this sort of expectation was not unusual with work addicts.

Opening the door to my office, I said, "I'm sorry, but I have another client coming in just a few minutes, and I can't disrespect her time by extending your session because you were late. As I said, your scheduled session is now over. I will be more than happy to set up another time for you to come in." Looking first dejected and then annoyed, Betty pulled her phone out of her purse, dialed a number, and started to walk out of the office. As she began talking, I looked at Lucas and said, "Regardless of what Betty does or doesn't do, I'm hoping you will continue your sessions. You have a lot to learn about work addiction. And cut down on that gum. You're a nicotine addict."

The Various Faces of Work

According to a 2004 Gallup poll, close to half of working Americans put in 35 to 44 hours on the job per week. Then there are the more compulsive ones. Over a quarter of us (26 percent) work 45 to 59 hours, while 12 percent work 60 or more. And every once in a while, most of us find ourselves needing to put in a few more hours—to make some extra cash, catch up on projects, impress the boss, or tackle a new challenge. Or we may be saving to start a business of our own.

For many of us, our career partially defines how we feel about ourselves, especially when we achieve our goals or experience success. A good friend of mine is a housekeeper. When she is done cleaning a home from top to bottom, she sitd back, drinkd a soda, and admired her work. Many of us enjoy our work. Every occupation has its ups and downs, but most jobs also have tasks, associations, challenges, and activities that keep us engaged and interested. If it isn't for the creative challenge, maybe we love our job because of the money we make. A number of us might like who we work with, or we enjoy the freedom of being our own boss. But regardless of how we feel about our job, work is just one fraction of our identity. To live a healthy, balanced life, we need family, friends, creative pursuits, hobbies, recreation, community, and relaxation in our day-to-day lives.

When long hours at work become a pattern, chances are there is a problem. A person who is a workaholic has difficulty putting the job aside when outside of work situations. This persistent need to work interferes with relationship needs, family, friendships, health needs, and leisure time. When we consistently allow our job to interfere with other areas of our lives, we create an imbalance. This loss of balance can create interpersonal difficulties and even health issues.

The Best-Dressed Addiction

Bryan Robinson, author of *Chained to the Desk,* believes work addiction is the "best-dressed addiction" because in our society we are rewarded for such behavior. Workaholics love talking about how hard they work, how busy they are, what they have accomplished, the money they have made, how in-demand their services are. And there are many payoffs for excessive working, such as bigger paychecks, power, promotions, prestige, and a sense of control. Because work addiction is a feel-good, look-good, socially acceptable behavior, partners often overlook the negative consequences and allow it to continue.

Workaholics come in many guises. There's the person who spends sixty hours per week at the office, making big deals, troubleshooting, and managing the lives of hundreds to thousands of others. In other cases, the office at home can see as much action as the office at work. These men and women always take tasks with them on vacation. They drag computers and cell phones to tropical islands and on cruises. Regularly excusing themselves from dinners, birthdays, holidays, school plays, anniversaries, family gatherings, and conversations with friends to attend to work-related issues after work hours, they rarely experience true intimacy with loved ones.

I've also clinically assisted workaholics—when they drop their work to show up for therapy, that is!—who put in long hours without any extra reward in their paychecks. These folks are rewarded with lots of atta-boy, atta-gal strokes and believe they are the only ones who can fulfill all work-related responsibilities. They also expect those who are working with them or for them to labor as hard as they do. Like alcoholics who put the bottle before all else, these "busy-addicts" see themselves as "human doings," not human beings.

I've heard work-obsessed professional belittle peers who maintain a balanced, forty-hour work week, commenting on their laziness or slacking off, not carrying their weight or being a team player. Such people often don't set aside time for medical, dental, and therapy visits because they believe they don't have even a moment to spare for such things. (Or if they do schedule an appointment, they're likely to cancel or not show up.) Because their own lives revolve around constant work or activity, they expect their partners and family to accommodate.

The workplace isn't the only cauldron brewing up workaholic behavior. There is the retiree who has joined numerous nonprofit organizations in town, filling up every minute of the day. His wife always believed that once he retired he'd spend more time with her, but she finds him home even less during these "golden years." He is on several boards for United Way organizations, volunteers at the local shelter, serves on church committees, and finds time to take meals to the elderly and sick in his community. He rarely takes time for recreation and is often too busy to see the grandkids.

And think of the perfectionist soccer moms and baseball coach dads who insist that every nook and cranny of their lives, and their children's lives, be rigidly scheduled and choreographed. I always feel uncomfortable around them, because neither they nor their kids ever take any time out to simply relax and unwind. The youngsters don't ever get to just play. If the parents who perpetuate this sort of lifestyle complain that their lives are too busy because of their children's activities, they probably don't recognize that they are exhausting their poor kids and using these activities to fuel their own drives and fulfill their own needs.

The Work Addict "Buzz"

More than twenty years ago, a few of us clinicians started to notice that workaholics and "busy addicts" don't have to ingest drugs or alcohol to change the way they feel. Instead, they use their own body chemistry to achieve this mood change. This behaviorally induced physiological change, combined with a powerful need to be loved and accepted for being a superachiever, creates a potent mood alteration that is extremely addictive.

Workaholism is a form of stress addiction—in other words, adrenaline addiction. Work addicts pump adrenaline through their bodies with compulsive busy behavior. This physiological chemical change counters depression and distances addicts from strong emotions. It numbs an array of painful feelings, old and new.

Adrenaline is a hormone, a part of the body's natural defense mechanism. When we are stressed, frightened, or feeling intense emotions such as anger or fear, our body increases adrenaline production so that we can quickly make decisions about how to act to protect ourselves: the "fight or flight" response. Workaholics become addicted to the adrenaline rush that accompanies the intensity of tasks involving creating and controlling, troubleshooting and problem-solving, challenges and pressures, conflict and competition—perhaps all on deadline.

An addiction to the pleasurable buzz induced by adrenaline is as powerful as alcoholism or drug addiction. The only difference is that many of the social consequences for work addiction are positive. Still, workaholism can destroy relationships as surely as chemical dependence can.

As a partner of a workaholic, you might be noticing some of these tendencies:

- Your partner pulls away from you at times, distancing him or herself because of work or other "busy-ness." Even when at home and physically available, your partner may not be emotionally available to you and other family members.

- Because of work, your partner consistently misses activities that are important to you and your children (school events, for example).

- Work seems to be more important to your partner than you are; your life seems to rotate around the partner's work schedule. You often change your own agenda or postpone activities to accommodate it.

- Your partner's work interferes with social commitments, and you find yourself making excuses for this.

- You feel judged by your partner for not working as hard or as many hours as he or she does, and your partner seems to feel unappreciated if you question those hours.

- You feel guilty when your partner tells you that long work hours pay the bills, and because of that paycheck you hesitate to ask for more of the partner's time.

- You feel neglected and lonely, but feel shamed when you ask for more time or attention from your partner.

If you are concerned about your own work or "busy addiction," or if you have a history with partners who show signs of it, take a look at the test in the chapter 6 worksheet in appendix A.

Work addiction can drive a solid wedge between couples, making intimacy and emotional connection almost impossible. Workaholism is a powerful, mood-altering addiction and the chase for this adrenaline rush can become more important to the addict than relationships, family, and friends. Work addiction is a cover for feelings and issues in need of resolution, such as low self-esteem, depression, communication difficulties, intimacy issues, past losses, and relationship conflict.

What Can I Do?

Work addicts and their partners can get help. With the following steps below, healing relationships can begin.

If you are the partner of a workaholic:

• Stop letting your life revolve around your partner's workaholic schedule or "busy" behavior.

• Don't buy into your partner's excuses about excessive work, and quit making excuses for your partner when family activities or social obligations are missed because of it.

• Know that it's still okay for you to rest and relax on your time off, even if your partner brings work home or takes it on vacation.

• Lower your expectations and don't wait for your partner to meet all your needs. If you are lonely, find friends and supports that can be there for you in a healthy, nurturing way.

• Stop enabling work addict behavior: don't pick up the slack and take on more of your partner's duties or obligations because of that person's long hours and preoccupation with work or "busyness."

• Understand that your partner's work addiction is not your fault, but that you are probably enabling it and it's your responsibility to learn how to quit.

If you are a workaholic yourself:

• Get the facts about your addiction.

• Understand that despite its many seeming rewards (paychecks, creative accomplishment, successful problem-solving, pats on the back, promotions), workaholism is a physically and emotionally destructive addiction to adrenaline. It exacts a high price in your personal life.

• Recognize that although you are not ingesting drugs or alcohol, you are forcing your body to manufacture large quantities of adrenaline to support the high you are addicted to.

• Connect with other individuals who have worked toward recovering from workaholism.

• Find a therapist or marriage counselor who understands workaholism.

Work addicts and their family members can also join support groups such as Workaholics Anonymous, Debtors Anonymous, Co-Dependents Anonymous,Al-Anon, or Adult Children of Alcoholics. (Many workaholics and their partners have grown up in families with addictions or losses that have never been healed.)

If you have a history of relationships with work-addicted partners, read the rest of the book for more assistance. You deserve a partner who is emotionally available, but for this to happen you need to understand why you've attracted addicted people up to now.

• • •

7

Sexual Obsessions, Cybersex, and Addiction: Distancing from Intimate Relationships with Fantasy

There's nothing better than good sex. But bad sex?
A peanut butter and jelly sandwich is better than bad sex.

— BILLY JOEL, SINGER-SONGWRITER

Playboy and *Hustler* have been around for decades, but erotic depictions have been around longer than that. Some of the first pornography can be found in Paleolithic cave paintings and carvings. In order words, we humans have been looking at pornography for millions of years! Fast-forward to the new millennium, with personal computers, the Internet, and Technology has opened up new avenues for pornography.

Sex is natural and fun. The act of sex sends hormones galore racing through our bodies and triggers pleasure centers in the brain. Experimenting with sex is also common. But when our behaviors around sexuality become excessive and interfere with other areas of our lives, the experimenting has moved from normal to abnormal. It has crossed the line and become an addiction.

According to noted psychologist Patrick Carnes, founder of the sexual addictions treatment movement and author of numerous best-selling books on the topic, "Sexual addiction is defined as any sexually-related, compulsive behavior which interferes with normal living and causes severe stress on family, friends, loved ones, and one's work environment." This definition—and more on Dr. Carnes's impressive work—can be found on his Web site, SexHelp.com (www.sexhelp.com/addiction_definitions.cfm).

Over the last few decades, more information has begun to surface on sexual addiction. No longer is it seen as a disorder related to only extreme acting out, as with sexual abuse or rape. Clinicians have identified milder versions of the disorder—but in any form, to any degree, sexual addiction affects the addict's ability to perceive the world realistically. Most important, the disorder has specific characteristics and behaviors that interfere with the ability to establish healthy, intimate relationships with self or others.

Sex addicts believe that a partner should physically appear as a sexual fantasy at all times. If I always need to have sex with vision of perfection, I can't have anything more than superficial encounters, because they will lack honesty and authenticity. Men and women from all walks of life who are afraid of true emotional connectedness often act out by seeking anonymous fantasy relationships online; visiting strip clubs and adult bookstores; engaging in emotional affairs without sex, in sex with prostitutes or one-night stands, or in sexual teasing with someone other than a partner; or masturbating compulsively. Sexual addicts can also become physiologically and psychologically addicted to the adrenaline and sex hormones that are produced by highly ritualized patterns of sexual behavior and obsessive imagining.

At the core of sexual addiction is intimacy phobia, or an inability to fully and honestly connect emotionally with another person. People avoid intimacy by keeping secrets, avoiding conflict, presenting only a "public" side, telling people only what they want to hear to avoid rejection, and not allowing themselves to appear vulnerable. Telling someone how we feel, when we feel it, in a way that is respectful to us and our partner, brings us closer. It builds trust, honesty, and a bond that can grow so strong and become so fulfilling that there is no need or room for addiction. (See the chapter 7 worksheet in appendix A to read about intimacy-avoiding tactics.)

What Happens to the Partners of Sex Addicts?

Partners of sexual addicts often notice distancing behavior from their partner, unexplained spending, unusual absences, and either a lack of sexual interest or an dramatic increase in need for sex on the part of the partner. Partners of sex addicts may begin to question their self-worth and their sanity. Feelings of anxiety, shame, depression, confusion, and loneliness are common.

I have often heard clients make comments like these:

- "If only we could have more good sex, we'd have a perfect relationship."

- "Before the kids were born, you really put energy into our sex life. You were in better shape, and you weren't so exhausted."

- "If you really loved me, you would try harder. Then I wouldn't have to read pornography or go to strip clubs."

- "If you were thinner, or made more money, I wouldn't have affairs."

- "Sex with you five times a week isn't enough. I need more sex."

- "You don't excite me anymore. I can really talk to him, and he cares."

- "How can I feel sexual with someone who complains because I don't help with chores or buy a bigger house?"

- "You expect me to give you sex when you cut off the credit card?"

- "If you would just get off my back about the time I spend with my buddies or girlfriends, our sex life would improve!"

- "If you loved me, you would participate in the sex acts I need, even if you don't especially like it or it scares you."

Though sexuality plays a major role in our intimate relationships, it is self-centered to expect Hollywood-style fantasy sex with a partner who never complains, has moments of sadness, who gets tired, ages, has bad days, says no, gains weight, works hard, gets angry, or needs to attend to other life chores. As relationships mature, it's rare to role-play sex games every other day or constantly be the fantasy partner. Hot sex at the drop of a hat seven days a week or more happens at the beginning of a relationship, but naturally decreases over time. In healthy relationships, sex is great fun but each partner acknowledges other responsibilities, activities, and interests.

If the co-addict or partner is a rape victim or has a history of sexual abuse either in childhood or in previous relationships, living with a sex addict will pull to the surface any unresolved emotions associated with these experiences. Even if the sex addiction is acted out in secret, the co-addict will still sense that something is not right. As anxiety increases, body perception issues will become stronger. *Unhealthy, inaccurate body perception difficulties are typically manifested as eating addictions or disorders. To this day, I have not met one co-addict of a sexual addict who does not have some sort of body perception issue.*

A New Venue

Computers, iPods, and cell phones have changed every area of our lives, mine included. My daily sunrise routine includes not only brushing my teeth, reading the newspaper, and walking my big old shaggy dog, but spending time with my computer. In fact, the computer comes first. Every morning, after rolling out of bed and sliding my feet into a ratty pair of green bedroom slippers, I grab a cup of hot green tea and head to my office.

With the push of a button, I'm connected to the Internet universe. My cyberspace fingers reach out to other professionals living as far away as Australia, not to mention numerous relatives, friends, and clients. Everyone in my life is wired in to my computer, making communication, business, relationships, and contact with loved ones just a keystroke away. With the click of a mouse, computers may have made our interactions more convenient. But the buffer of cyberspace can take away the feelings of intimacy experienced with face-to-face chats.

Computers not only buffer us from face to face contact, they can provide complete anonymity. So even though I'm sitting in my ugly brown terry cloth bathrobe, with my hair standing up on end, to the clients receiving my e-mail, I'm Carla Wills-Brandon the therapist. Such anonymity can be handy, but for many Internet users the anonymity of cyberspace can be a safe dwelling—perhaps too safe.

The lonely woman who feels poorly about herself can be vivacious and beautiful in a chat room. Flirting freely with numerous males in these cyberspace meeting halls can be a heady, mood-altering escape for the woman who typically feels unattractive and undesirable. The man who finds face-to-face relationships difficult can be the life of the party in cyberspace. If he finds he feels rejected or loses interest, there are no long, drawn-out goodbyes to contend with. All he needs to do is click "close" and visit another message board, Web site, or chat room.

Computers, chat rooms, and online dating services bring us an opportunity to meet people and express ourselves as we've never been able to before. Developing an online cyberspace personality can let us play out various fantasy roles. Though these online relationships are void of true intimacy, the thrill of fantasy can offer a temporary escape from life's everyday problems, difficulties, and disappointments. Internet addiction, or surfing the Web obsessively for hours on end, and excessive online gambling also serve this purpose, but for some thrill-seeking Internet users, cyberspace has even replaced the bedroom as a place to have sex.

What Is Cybersex?

Cybersex comes in a variety of forms, from the comical cartoon nudity to the posted photos of individuals engaged in hardcore sex acts. Cybersex videos can also be downloaded from the Internet. Along with this, it's possible to view live sex acts from the comfort of the living room, without ever having to leave the house for a strip club. Clicking on to take a peek every now and then isn't viewed by mental health professionals as a psychological difficulty. Cybersex is seen as an addiction when the short visits become longer and longer, interfering with other areas of life. These addicts unconsciously spend hours online.

Cybersex researcher and author Dr. Kimberly Young, executive director of the Center for Internet Addiction Recovery, describes the subject broadly on the Center's Web site (www.netaddiction.com/cyber-sexual_addiction.htm).

> Cybersex/Pornography Addiction is a specific sub-type of Internet addiction. Estimates suggest that 1 in 5 Internet addicts are engaged in some form of online sexual activity (primarily viewing cyberporn and/or engaging in cybersex). Studies show that men are more likely to view cyberporn, while women are more likely to engage in erotic chat. People who suffer from low self-esteem, a distorted body image, untreated sexual dysfunction, or a prior sexual addiction are more at risk to develop cybersex/cyberporn addictions. In particular, sex addicts often turn to the Internet as a new and safe sexual outlet to fulfill their underlying compulsive habit.

With the privacy of cybersex, the shy woman who has always been interested in sexual adventuring can instantly find erotica dedicated to bisexuality, sex with multiple partners, sex rooms with video catering to dominating or submissive tastes. The man who fears disease or risk from acting out sexually with prostitutes or strip-club dancers can quickly access a variety of sites dedicated to such stimulation. No longer does one have to sneak into the local movie rental business to pick up pornographic films or cautiously tiptoe around a bookstore looking for the sexy magazine wrapped in cellophane. Sexual activity is found indiscriminately in cyberspace.

When my son was twelve, he punched into his search engine the name of a famous female teen idol. Before we knew it we were both looking at a nude picture of a voluptuous blonde! Let's just say that night we had a long mother-son discussion about healthy sexuality. Several months later, my eight-year-old son went scouting the Web for a certain comic book and oh no! There we were again. Same nude pose, but this time the well-endowed creature's face was framed in long brunette curls. Joshua's eyes grew to the size of saucers. Then he broke into hysterical laughter: "Look, Mommy! She doesn't have any clothes!"

I'm not making light of computer pornography here, I'm just acknowledging that for many people, a little fantasy now and then is not a problem. Couples in my practice have often joked about visiting these sites together just to see what's out there. Single men and women looking for a quick sexual release have also admitted to me that they have periodically visited these sites. Once they become involved in a meaningful relationship, they no longer needed such stimulation.

But of course not everyone visiting these sites takes a quick peek and moves on. Some people become obsessed with pornography. In these situations, cybersex has replaced meaningful relationships and time spent online detracts from other life activities.

Obsession with cyberspace is a new millennium problem. For some Internet users it's as addictive as cocaine, as powerful as alcohol is for the alcoholic, and as financially devastating as is compulsive gambling. An obsession with computer sex destroys intimacy in our primary relationships. It's the secret no one wants to talk about, but as a professional, I see it time and time again.

Cyberspace Obsessions

In our waiting room, Michael and I greeted the couple arriving for a joint marital session. Jeff and Marie had been married for twenty-five years. Both were professionals, and their two daughters were in college. In her late forties, Marie was attractive, obviously took very good care of her physical self, and carried herself with confidence. Jeff was in his early fifties, also in very good shape. He was a daily runner, and only the gray at his temples suggested his true age. Looking at this couple, no one would ever suspect that all was not well in their marriage.

After entering my office, Marie sat down gracefully and crossed her long legs. Jeff sat next to her and took her hand, but she quickly withdrew from his touch. Michael gave me a knowing nod, and both of us could see we had a powder keg situation in front of us.

Marie had initially come to see me because she was concerned about sex. Sexual relations had all but ceased between her and Jeff. When she asked her husband why sex between them was at an all-time low, he attributed it to stress on the job and assured her it would pass. Nine months later, it still had not passed She wondered if he was having an affair and spent months spying on him, trying to catch him in the act. She knew something was up, felt it in her gut, but couldn't put her finger on it. When Jeff wasn't looking, Marie would search his briefcase, check his wallet, sniff his shirts for someone else's perfume, but time and time again would come up empty-handed.

During one of her briefcase searches, Marie stumbled upon a credit card account she was unfamiliar with. She and Jeff usually reviewed their bills together, so she was taken aback to discover that not only did he have a credit card she was not familiar with but that it was being sent to a post office box she had never heard of. The charges made on the credit card were consistent, but it was difficult to determine just what these charges were for. When she confronted her husband, he assured her that the credit card charges were for the office, and though her gut told her he was not being truthful, she accepted his answer.

About a month later, all hell broke loose. After a long day at the office, Marie decided to go to bed earlier than usual. As she kissed her husband goodnight, she asked, "What are you planning to do this evening?" He replied, "I've got some work to do on the computer. I'll be to bed shortly."

After several hours of sleep, Marie awoke from restless dreaming. The stress of the day was impinging on her sleep, and she thought maybe a cup of herbal tea would relax her. After brewing up some sweet chamomile, she saw the light on in the computer room and decided to surprise Jeff with a middle-of-the-night romantic rendezvous. Jeff was not prepared for her visit. Quietly slipping into the room, Marie found him sitting in front of the computer nude, a graphic live sex act on the screen. It was obvious that Jeff was masturbating. Feeling physically sick, Marie quickly left the room, asking herself, "Why doesn't he just ask to have sex with me?"

The next morning, Jeff tried to explain to Marie that what she saw him doing rarely happened. He quickly added that he had stumbled upon the pornographic site while doing office work and that the graphic scenes had naturally aroused him. After dressing for work, he kissed her good-bye and left for the office. Marie had an hour to spare, so once she was sure Jeff was on the road, she quickly went to the computer and turned it on. Searching his files, she found nothing that could be related to pornographic material. After an hour or so, Marie decided she had overreacted. She was about to shut down the computer when an e-mail came in. It advertised a pornographic Web site. After clicking on the site's homepage address, Marie felt dazed. There on the screen, looking back at her seductively, was a picture of the woman she had seen nude on the screen when she had walked in on Jeff the previous night.

Moving her mouse to "History," she then clicked to see what other sites had been visited over the last week. The nauseated feeling returned as she examined the sites listed. As she clicked each one on, she discovered the majority of them were pornographic sites, most requiring a credit card payment for access. Marie was devastated.

During the marital therapy session, Marie read a letter to Jeff describing her feelings about his sexual acting out with computer porn. She had thought the lack of sexual intimacy was her fault, and it hurt her to believe she was no longer sexually desirable to Jeff. Fearing that he found her physically unattractive, she had gone on a strict diet, lost weight, bought sexy lingerie, and had even considered plastic surgery, hoping this would please him. Sadly, her attempts at enticing him seemed to go unnoticed.

Now Marie broke down, turned to Jeff, and cried, "Did you ever even notice me? Did you ever see how hard I was trying to please you?" Jeff seemed surprised. Drying her tears, Marie added that she had felt depressed, lonely, confused, and older than her years. Her obsession with trying to attract him sexually had interfered with other areas of her life. Her business had suffered, as she had difficulty staying focused and on track. Even their two daughters had noticed she was on edge and preoccupied. Once again, Jeff appeared confused. Turning to Michael, he asked, "How can looking at a little porn on the computer have created so much chaos? Her feeling this way, you can't really blame that on me." With this statement, Jeff had exposed the depth of his addiction. Whenever we find we need to minimize or lie about our behavior, chances are something is wrong.

With Jeff's words, Marie's tears returned. As I looked at her, it was obvious that all signs of confidence were gone. Her self-esteem had been crushed. The graceful, successful businesswoman who had initially walked through the door of my office was nowhere to be found. Instead, here sat an insecure wife who believed she was sexually unattractive to her husband. Filled with hurt, pain, and rage, she turned to him and cried, "How can I compete with perfectly sculptured twenty-something fantasies on those porn sites?" Then she looked at me and asked, "How can I measure up to that?"

Understanding the Affair with Internet Porn

When does a person cross the line from having occasional sexual fun online to becoming a cybersex addict? When the time spent surfing porn sites interferes with a person's intimate relationships with partners, family, and friends. In some cases this addiction can also have financial, legal, health and work-related consequences. Like alcohol and drugs, cybersex addiction can become the ultimate mood-altering escape. Instead of dealing with life on life's terms—processing feelings, resolving problems, and addressing relationship conflicts, insecurities, loneliness, grief, or anger—some people use online sex as a temporary fix. And in excess, this superficial sex eventually undermines primary relationships. If a person is getting every emotional, physical and sexual need taken care of online with fantasy relationships, there is no need to put forth effort at making real, here-and-now relationships work. There is no need to work on problems, misunderstandings, miscommunications, hurt feelings, sexual issues, and relationship conflicts.

Such an obsession is somewhat analogous to an extramarital affair, only in this situation the affair is not physically with another person but with the images on a screen or with chat room participants. And a fantasy lover can be the perfect lover. Such a lover does not talk back, argue, cry, express hurt feelings, say no to certain sex acts, demand compromise, or ask that feelings or needs be heard.

Online fantasy lovers are paid to provide a service, to be a fantasy. They will say or even do whatever is required by the person paying for the service. Online sexual personas have no true voice at all. The user, feeling a sense of control, can imagine whatever he or she likes. Chat room chatters can simply "delete" an online love affair if the going gets tough, too demanding, or if a fantasy is not being fulfilled. Marie is right. How can a real breathing person compete with such instant, risk-free gratification?

But because the secret act is not happening physically between two people in a motel bed, it is often hard for the cybersex-obsessed to see the damage occurring. The person is blind to how it is undermining their own relationship.

Justifications and Denial

Regular cybersex surfers tend to have some common rationalizations and excuses. In my practice, I've often heard justifications like these.

"I'm not cheating on my partner by looking at porno sites or going to chat rooms. There's nothing wrong with looking at pornography or having a little sexual fantasy fun. I'm not having actual sex with someone."

A quick peek every now and then is not a problem, but many porn surfers eventually find that they are spending more and more time on it. One client of mine was amazed after realizing he'd been porn surfing for four hours. "I couldn't believe I lost that much time surfing these sites. That's half my workday!" Sexual stimulation on the Net can begin to replace healthy sex with a partner. And the act of porn cruising or chatting with online lovers may actually increase the body's production of the lust hormone phenylethylamine. Cybersex addicts get hooked on these lust hormones, not only on the ones associated with sexual release.

One woman I worked with found that she lost business contacts because she had spent her whole day online surfing porn sites. As she said, "It was like I was on drugs." Imagine her surprise when I told her she actually was on a mood-altering chemical. Another woman neglected her children while chatting with a cyberlover. When her kids needed her attention, she became angry and frustrated. Excessive cybersex not only takes the place of healthy sex but also interferes with everyday activities and relationships.

"Cybersex is better than cheating on my partner."

Excessive cybersex *is* cheating on a partner. If an Internet porn cruiser is getting all of his or her sexual needs taken care of online, there is no incentive to connect with a partner. Husbands, wives, and significant others feel this distancing and often wonder why they are sensing detachment in the relationship. In my practice, the partners of those involved with excessive cybersex truly believe that the distance they are feeling from their loved one is somehow their fault. They think, "If I were prettier, slimmer, taller, younger, better endowed, a better lover, made more money, had a different hair color, my partner would pay more attention to me." They tend to make the distancing behavior about them, when in reality it is more about their partner's difficulty with intimacy. Fantasy is easier than face-to-face intimacy. My cybersex cruising clients are always shocked to hear that their behavior is actually undermining their primary relationship.

"My partner isn't in a sexual mood tonight, and I am. So I'm just getting my needs taken care of. If my partner took care of me better, I wouldn't need porn."

Because Internet porn cruising can often be done at varied times and in secret, partners are often unaware of the extent of it. And with fantasy pornography, cybersex users can control the situation and call the shots. Intimate risk-taking and vulnerability do not need to be experienced. On the other hand, making a date to have sex—intimate, loving, respectful sex with a live, feeling, opinionated partner—takes work! Many of us don't know how to talk about sex, ask for sexual activity, say no to certain acts of sex, or work through sexual issues. Turning to superficial cybersex keeps us from addressing these issues. Again, as long as sexual needs are being taken care of online, there is little incentive to reach out to a partner and work things out.

"I don't know why my partner is so angry. At least I'm not having sex outside the relationship. Getting my extra need for sexual gratification online keeps me from risking sexually transmitted diseases."

It also limits intimacy. The act of sex can be just that—the act of sex. Every once in a while, having sex just to "get our rocks off" isn't such a bad thing. This is adolescent sexuality and is more about release than intimacy. Though such periodic release is normal, it must be balanced with healthy adult sexuality.

With mature sexuality, the act of sex is about interfacing and connecting with another person on a very intimate, loving level, with respect, care, concern, and compromise. With cybersex, sex is only about fantasy and release. In other words, what we are talking about here is a form of adolescent sexuality. The attitude here is, "My good feelings about sex and who I am are based on what you can do for me." Excessive cybersex cheapens our true adult sexual relationships.

Let's return to Jeff and Marie's situation. As you will see, several years of excessive cybersex has stunted Jeff's intimacy development.

Illusionary Love: The Symptoms and the Price

Jeff and Marie sat quietly as Michael gave them some information on the consequences relationships suffer with excessive cybersex. Suddenly, a wave of relief seemed to wash over Marie. "So I'm not crazy?" she said. "It's not me? I've been feeling nuts for months." Turning to Jeff, she asked, "How long have you been into pornography?"

Jeff looked at Michael with confusion. "Don't all guys get into pornography?" he asked. "I thought it was a rite of passage. I've had porn since I was a teen. I think of it as normal. Why should Net porn be any different?" Michael replied, "Jeff, how would you feel about looking at a guide that lists some of the possible symptoms of excessive online sexual acting out?"

Identifying the Signs

Indentifying and treating excessive cybersex is a fairly new field of study for helping professionals. Thankfully, a few mental health specialists have courageously taken a stab at defining this disorder. Robert Weiss, a clinician in California, has compiled a useful guide to help people know whether they have crossed the line from fun to cybersex addiction. Robert has been supported by Patrick Carnes and his guide is very useful in assisting couples confronted with this particular intimacy block. The guide is reprinted with permission from Robert Weiss in the chapter 7 worksheet in appendix A. Take a look and see if you can relate to any of the suggested symptoms.

After Jeff answered the questions from Robert Weiss's Cybersex Addiction Screening Test (C-SAST), Michael scored his responses. Jeff had more than three positive responses, indicating he had issues with cybersex addiction. "I feel sick," he sighed after reviewing his results. "I had no idea cybersex had become such a problem. I guess it has taken over my life," he added. Looking at his answers, Jeff seemed defeated. "Okay, I admit I go online every day, sometimes twice a day. Yeah, I've kind of known it's a problem for some time, but I didn't know how to talk about it. Where do we go from here?"

What Can We Do?

If you are a single person and you have discovered that excessive cybersex is keeping you from dating or having meaningful relationships, you may want to seek out support and further education from confidential groups such as Sex Addicts Anonymous. Such groups can also be found online: see the "Sexual Healing" section in appendix B: "Self-Help Resources." There, and in this book's bibliography, you will also find numerous books on the subject of sexual compulsivity. Arming yourself with information about cybersex addiction is an extremely important step. Once it's confirmed that the line has been crossed, and involvement has moved from a smidgen of fantasy to obsessive acting out, it becomes difficult to repeat the behavior over and over again without seeing the negative consequences.

Healing from excessive cybersex in a relationship takes both partners. Both partners must look at their inability to communicate honestly in their relationship, and both must take steps to begin healing from this intimacy block.

For those obsessed with cybersex, these steps are worth considering:

1. Get honest about how often you use the Web for sex.

2. Notice how Web sex feels emotionally safer than sex with a partner.

3. Examine if cybersex has become a reward or a way to avoid strong feelings or to escape the realities of life.

4. Notice whether abstaining from cybersex for one to two weeks produces irritation, agitation, anxiety, depression, rage, or a sense of emptiness.

5. Connect with other people who have discovered they are addicted to sex on the Web. Support groups such as Sex and Love Addicts Anonymous (SLAA) or Sex Addicts Anonymous (SAA) can reduce the shame you have about being caught up in this obsession.

For partners of those obsessed with cybersex:

1. Understand that you are not responsible for your partner's acting out with cybersex, but that you are enabling it out by keeping it secret or denying to yourself that it's a problem. In so doing, you are a part of the problem.

2. It is not your job to block cybersex sites from your partner's computer, nor is it your job to feel guilty about financial problems resulting from your partner's cybersex expenses.If you scrimp on grocery, medical, or other bills to help the cybersex-obsessed person pay off that debt, you are still serving as an enabler.

3. Your hair color, age, and height are not the problem. Your less than "perfect" body or job has not forced your mate to be involved with pornographic sites or chat rooms.

4. Start trusting your gut feelings. If your intuition tells you your partner is acting out with cybersex, chances are that he or she has done so within the last twenty-four hours.

5. Know that you need to be involved in a support group such as Sex and Love Addicts Anonymous (SLAA) or COSA, for those

recovering from codependencies in this area. These group meetings can provide you with a safe place to talk about cybersex in your relationship.

Healing Is Possible

Jeff and Marie agreed to begin attending support groups and reading books on cybersex addiction. Jeff also contracted to abstain from computer use for thirty days. When he needed to contact clients for work purposes, he used the telephone or pulled out his typewriter. Marie agreed to leave his cybersex Web sites alone, and eventually Jeff blocked them himself. Both Jeff and Marie abstained from all sex for two months. Instead, they went out on dates with hand-holding and kissing. Because sex was not being used to "fix" relationship problems or feelings, they were both forced to begin working out some of their relationship issues. Eventually, they came for another therapy session.

That day, Jeff and Marie walked into the office and sat down. They were holding hands. Today's session was going to be rough, and they knew it. Marie and Jeff had resumed sexual relations, but they were having difficulty talking about it. In spite of this, they were committed to doing what was necessary to work things out. Based on years of professional experience, Michael and I knew that as long as the two of them were willing to do the necessary work, true intimacy would blossom.

• • •

8

Am I Hungry or Am I Hurting? Intimacy Dysfunction and Food Addiction Issues

I'm not going to have sex while I am fat . . .
It's probably not right. I should probably be happy with the way I look
and happy with the way my body is and happy that someone would
want to have sex with me, but I'm not.

— KIRSTIE ALLEY, ACTRESS

I looked at my clock and saw that Andrea was already twenty minutes late for her appointment. "This is not like her," I said to myself. I'd been working with Andrea for several months, and she was always on time. When she discovered that her latest lover was having sexual affairs with several other women, she had sought out my help.

Randy wasn't the only partner to cheat on her. When Andrea married her husband Donald, she thought all her dreams had come true. Donald was a talented young musician, and during the early years Andrea supported him both emotionally and financially. When a music venture didn't pan out, Donald would be devastated, but Andrea always cheered him on by telling him success was just around the corner. He started writing music lyrics for the film industry and finally hit the big time. With this success, they finally had a net under their financial tightrope. The couple agreed Andrea would quit working and devote her time to raising their young daughter, Rose.

As Donald's career continued to take off, he and Andrea began receiving some great perks. They were invited to all the "right" parties with all the "right" people. With these new connections, they were able to enroll Rose into an exclusive school, and Andrea now had time for her painting. It had been years since she had pulled out her watercolors and paintbrushes; she'd been working such long days just to put food on the table. Now, with her daughter in school, Andrea finally had a few hours to devote to herself and her art.

For a year or so life seemed good, but as Donald neared forty, something started to change. First, sex became an issue. Donald didn't seem interested in making love. Andrea eventually discovered he was pleasuring himself sexually with pornographic magazines, a fact that left her feeling unattractive and aged. She tried new hairstyles, lost a few pounds, replaced her beloved "hippie" wardrobe with a more youthful look, and even went out and bought several cute lacy nightgowns. Sadly, nothing seemed to work, and she found herself wondering, "How can I compete with the sexy women in those glossy magazines?"

As time went on, their sex life tapered off to almost nothing, and Andrea questioned herself more and more. She would cook Donald his favorite meal, light candles, and sit waiting for him to come home to her, but instead he often called to say he'd be late. He'd also started going out to lunch, dinner, or parties with movie people or other musicians without Andrea. "Am I an embarrassment?" she asked herself. She knew she wasn't as polished as many of Donald's new friends, but everyone had always told her she was fun to be around.

Andrea knew she was putting on a little extra weight, and though she tried to watch what she ate, she found when sitting home alone that certain foods gave her immense comfort. Looking at herself in the mirror she often thought, "Who on earth could compete with the model-thin female musicians Donald surrounds himself with? I'm forty, so I'm going to look a little more rounded!" Sometimes she and her daughter Rose had junk food nights: dinner might be banana splits or pancakes with whipped cream. At first this was fun, but she knew these food festivals weren't going to fill up the emptiness she was feeling—and they wouldn't replace the fathering Rose desperately needed. Andrea felt very lonely, and playing both mother and father to her daughter was becoming more and more difficult.

After a few months, Andrea finally confronted Donald about why he was never home. He responded with, "Well, someone needs to make a living around here. I don't see you doing much of anything." Stunned, Andrea said, "We had agreed I would stay at home and take care of our daughter. Don't you remember the long hours I worked to pay for your music school? I thought we had an understanding." Hurt, she left the room and went to the kitchen to bake a cake. Andrea had promised her daughter she would bring her famous three-layer chocolate cream cheese cake to the school open house that evening.

After she put the cake in the oven, she went to find Donald. As usual he was on the phone and when he saw her, he waved her off. Feeling dejected, she thought, "I just don't seem to matter to him." Returning to the kitchen, Andrea began whipping up a fluffy chocolate frosting for the cake. As she took a lick off of the spoon to see how it tasted, Donald walked in and looking at her with disgust. "You're a bit out of shape," he said. "Do you really need to be eating that?" Feeling shamed, Andrea put the spoon in the kitchen sink. Donald then opened up the refrigerator, grabbed a bottle of water, and added, "You aren't taking care of yourself like you used to." Andrea was so hurt she was speechless. After strolling out of the kitchen, and then out of the house, Donald fired up his new motorcycle, and with that Andrea knew he wouldn't be going with her to their daughter's open house. That night at the school Andrea tasted every single dessert, twice.

Andrea eventually discovered that Donald wasn't always attending to business when he was away from home. Instead, he was kindling romances with several pretty, rail-thin female musicians, all much younger than Andrea, who now felt discarded at the age of forty-two. When she confronted him, Donald tried to blame her for the affairs. He calmly told her she wasn't as attractive to him sexually as she once had been, and added, "You don't appreciate or understand me like my music friends do."

Andrea wondered, "Am I the problem? Is it because of me that he had the affairs?" She went on a liquid diet, thinking if she lost weight it might rekindle the romance in their marriage. Several of her paintings had sold and she was getting good reviews from the art community, so she was also contributing financially. Andrea had even been asked to teach an art class at the local community college. In spite of this, Donald insisted she was the problem in the marriage. Distressed, Andrea accepted the blame, and her weight began to increase even more. Donald eventually divorced Andrea and quickly moved into an apartment with one of his young female musician friends. Watching all of this, Andrea felt just sick. She had devoted the first part of her adult life to supporting a man who had dropped her as soon as success allowed him to. What would she do with the second half of her life?

After being single for several years, Andrea lost the weight and then met Stan. He was a history teacher at the community college, and in the beginning they had a whirlwind romance. He thought she was sexy and intelligent and went out of his way to say so as often as possible. Six months into the relationship, Andrea noticed Stan wasn't complimenting her so often anymore. Like Donald, he too was starting to get on her about her weight. Stan even put together an exercise program for her. Grabbing Andrea's belly, he would say, "We need to do something about this!" A year into dating, she caught Stan in his office having sex with a student. Again, Andrea swore off men.

After that Andrea wouldn't even consider dating. Instead, she threw herself into motherhood and her art. She became a well-respected artist and regularly had shows in New York, Los Angeles, and even London. Andrea's weight started to create health issues for her, so she went into treatment for compulsive eating. While in treatment she worked on her anger toward Donald, Stan, and a few other unfaithful lovers. Andrea even explored the sexual abuse she had suffered at the hands of an uncle. In treatment she learned that people in need of healing from anorexia or bulimia were as unhappy as she was. She discovered that all food addicts abuse food and their bodies to avoid feeling emotions in desperate need of attention. Once out of treatment, Andrea was able to stick to a food plan, achieve a healthy weight, and return to the things she loved most—her daughter and her art.

While showing her latest watercolor collection in New York, Andrea met Randy. He too was an artist, and after several romantic dinners, they discovered they had a lot in common. Within a matter of weeks, Andrea was sexually involved with Randy. One evening while gazing into the eyes of her latest love over a candlelit supper, Andrea realized she couldn't even begin to eat the sumptuous pasta fettuccini dish sitting before her. Pinching herself, she thought, "True love has struck! Finally, I've found the man of my dreams. He won't hurt me."

The couple decided to combine their households and move in together in Andrea's home town. Rose was just finishing up her senior year, so they found a townhouse in a neighborhood close to her high school. Randy wasn't too happy about the location because it meant a longer commute to work for him. He also disliked Rose's big white tomcat Max, who slept where he pleased and was used to having the run of the house. Andrea discovered that Randy not only hated cats, but he was a neat freak, upset by any sort of mess. Having a teenage daughter, Andrea was used to seeing a sweatshirt on the couch or stack of books on the kitchen counter. Randy, who never had children of his own, told Andrea she had spoiled her daughter terribly and added, "I'm not going to tolerate what you consider to be normal teenage behavior." Within a few months he was pushing for Rose live with her father.

Soon Andrea started putting the weight back on. She'd been attending a support group for people with eating addictions, but had stopped after becoming involved with Randy. Andrea was no longer lunching with friends, either, and she'd put her watercolors and paint brushes back up on the shelf. Once again she was centering her life around a man, and this time Andrea was at risk not only for losing herself but her daughter Rose.

One afternoon Andrea decided to begin preparing for her daughter's graduation party by experimenting with a stuffed mushroom recipe. As she taste-tested the stuffing drizzled in melted butter, her daughter came into the kitchen and sat down. "Mom," Rose said, "I need to talk to you."

Her tone was serious, and Andrea knew something wasn't right. Putting the dressing aside, she wiped her hands on a dishtowel and sat down on a kitchen stool across from her daughter. "So serious!" Andrea said. "Are you nervous about graduation?"

"No Mom," Rose replied. "Actually, I can't wait to get out of here." Hurt, Andrea asked, "Why, honey? I thought you were going to live at home while you went to community college. What's changed?" Andrea could tell her daughter was uneasy and struggling to tell her something. "Go ahead, sweetie. You and I have always been honest with each other." After taking a deep breath, Rose said, "Okay, do you really want to know why I'm leaving? I can't deal with Randy. He's always on my case—not only about my cat, but everything. He doesn't like the way my bedroom is set up, he's upset if I leave my purse on a chair or a dish in the sink, and I feel like I can't breathe. I get As and Bs on my report card but he criticizes me for the Bs. I can't measure up to his ridiculous expectations. It's like living in a prison!" Andrea could see her daughter was almost in tears and reached over hug her. "Honey, you know he loves me, and he loves you too. He only wants what's best for us."

Pushing her mother away, Rose started crying angrily. "Are you that blind, Mom? You're miserable! He criticizes you constantly. You've given up your life, your friends, your art, and time with me for him, but it's still not enough." Andrea moved again to comfort her daughter. "Honey, it isn't that bad. I know we've had to make some changes, but things will smooth out. Try to be patient and you'll see. Everything will be all right. I promise." Shaking her head, Rose began walking away, but then she turned toward her mother and sadly said, "Maybe you want to live like this, but I can't. Haven't you noticed I never invite any of my friends over anymore?" Seeing her mother's look of surprise, Rose continued, "You've been so wrapped up in him, you didn't even notice, did you? Randy—your boyfriend—has been making inappropriate sexual remarks to my girlfriends. It's been so embarrassing!"

Shortly after Rose's graduation, Andrea realized that not only had Randy made sexual gestures toward her daughter's friends, he'd been having an affair with one of his old girlfriends. At first she was fearful of telling Randy she knew about the affair and was making arrangements for Rose to go live with her father, but something stopped her. Looking through an old photo album, she began to notice a pattern. Whenever Andrea started a new love affair she was always trim, in shape, and cheerful. As the relationships progressed, her pictures showed weight increase, depression, and unhappiness. Each of her partners had been sexually dysfunctional, and the more they acted out sexually, the more her weight increased. Andrea made an appointment to see me after reading my book, *Is It Love or Is It Sex? Why Relationships Don't Work.*

Over time she learned her food addiction was directly related not only to the sexual abuse she experienced as a child but to her relationships with sexually addicted men. Because of her abuse history, Andrea was attracted to partners who confused sexual fantasy with intimate love. When the relationships demanded realness and intimacy and she no longer measured up to the original superficial fantasy that once attracted her lovers, they were off looking for the drug of lust elsewhere. And when that happened, Andrea buried her pain with food.

Andrea finally arrived for her session a half-hour late, but when she walked through my office door, she was beaming. "I just kicked Randy out! I may be fat, but his affairs are not my fault! I finally get it. I need to work on me, not Randy, Donald, or Stan. If I do this, I'll finally have a decent relationship with a partner." Smiling at her, I closed the door and replied, "That's great news! Now we can really get to work!"

Eating Disorders and Intimacy

When faced with day-to-day life challenges, many of us find ourselves escaping by hanging out in front of the refrigerator looking for that mood-altering sugar or carbohydrate fix. Like alcohol, drug, work, sex, and gambling addictions, addictive eating is mood-altering, changing the way we feel. Eating additions help us to bury our feelings and, to some extent, have enabled us to function and survive in the world. Indeed, these addictions—including obsessive-compulsive eating, anorexia, bulimia, excessive exercising, and distorted body perception disorders—

usually result from practicing survival skills developed under stress. But over time, they also severely limit our ability to create a satisfying, healthy relationship with a partner. For more on these topics, see my earlier books, *Am I Hungry or Am I Hurting?* and *Eat Like a Lady: A Guide for Overcoming Bulimia.*

As a young bulimic I became a master at insulating myself from pain, shame, and other feelings by binging on large quantities of carbohydrates. I called my food addiction my "natural antidepressant." Binging increased my serotonin levels and temporarily countered depression. Addictive behavior with food allowed me to escape the difficult feelings I had as a child and young adult. By shielding me from reality, the bulimia provided me with a false sense of security. As with all dysfunctional survival skills, my eating addiction eventually backfired. While in addiction, I never learned how to live life in the real world. In essence, I never grew up.

Types of Eating Disorders

There are many kinds of eating disorders, but for now, let's look at three common types—compulsive overeating, bulimia, and anorexia nervosa— and their links with intimacy issues.

COMPULSIVE OVEREATING

Folks struggling with this addiction tend to be twenty or more pounds overweight. For many compulsive overeaters, the added weight keeps them from experiencing who they really are. The weight becomes a distraction that pushes other, more painful feelings and issues aside. Many compulsive eaters gain weight during or after a relationship with a sex addict. Though much of this is unconscious behavior, the result is an emotional numbing that walls off strong feelings. For the co-addict, little comes through these walls, and rarely does anything move out from behind them. It's like being enclosed in a cylinder, fearing what's outside. Food is used to medicate emotions in much the same way that alcohol soothes the alcoholic.

Compulsive eaters derive a false sense of security from food. The food numbs the pain and rage related to current relationship issues or past hurts, making us feel fine for the moment. But if we can't feel our pain, we can't heal it either. Until the eating addiction is addressed, it's difficult to fully see what is happening in a relationship. Eating addictions buffer us from the relationship dysfunction. With recovery, not only do we begin to feel better about ourselves, but we become aware of our relationship situation now that the buffer is gone. As self-esteem grows, confidence rises and boundaries can be set. Only then can current or future relationships can become more functional.

BULIMIA

Another common eating disorder, bulimia can often be found when sexual addiction is present in a relationship. This addiction involves bingeing on large amounts of food, be it carrots or cake, and then purging the body of the consumed calories by vomiting, using herbal or pharmaceutical laxatives or colonics, fasting, exercising excessively, or other means. Most bulimics are weight appropriate and appear self-confident. In reality, this false shell of security covers deep-seated pain, fear, rage, loneliness, and shame. Like compulsive overeaters, bulimics avoid the realities of life by altering painful feelings with food. Because both bingeing and purging are mood-altering, the addiction becomes a temporary problem-solver. The bulimic also has a distracting obsession with not gaining weight and with being in control.

Those suffering from this addictiongenerally believe that "if I appear perfect on the outside, maybe my inside feelings of pain and shame will be under control and go away." The function of the bingeing behavior is to cover up shame, but the emotional relief is only momentary. Bingeing actually increases shameful feelings, and then there is a need to purge those emotions away. So, like other addictions, bulimia boomerangs as a "fix." Bulimics are often masterful at pushing aside emotion related to relationship difficulties and other life challenges. Abstaining from the binge and purge cycle forces feelings to the surface. Once bulimia is in check, it's impossible to ignore relationship issues such as sex addiction and intimacy phobia.

ANOREXIA NERVOSA

Another addiction that can temporarily distract from past and present life difficulties, anorexia nervosa involves extreme weight loss, during which the sufferer believes nothing is wrong. Anorexics work toward perfecting their bodies, an obsession that turns into delusional body perception. In many cases sufferers continue to believe they are overweight when in reality they are emaciated. Malnourished anorexics create a chemical imbalance in the body that alters mood, a condition I call the "anorexic high." Because of the intense denial associated with this eating addiction, many anorexics have close brushes with death.

An anorexic's delusional thinking contributes to an inaccurate perception of life in general. The need to escape the realities of life indicates a strong desire for safety. The unconscious belief for the anorexic is, "If I'm in control, I can be safe in the world." By not seeing life as it really is, anorexics use this illusionary fantasy to push away the truth about relationship dysfunction and unresolved pain. Anorexics have damaged boundaries and tend to hook up with partners who may be sexual addicts.

The Link between Sex and Food Addiction in Couples

Many of us don't understand that it's okay to be imperfect. Unfortunately, the media bombards us with images of bodily perfection day in and day out. The constant visual barrage of flawless skin, sculpted bodies, and thick glossy hair presented in print and on screens can leave us feeling inadequate about who we are and how we look. When we feel that we can't measure up to these impossible standards we may use sex, food, or other addictions to mask our shame and low sense of self-worth.

While driving home from the office one evening, I was listening to a national radio talk show. The topic was infidelity, and a woman had called in to tell the host that she didn't blame her husband for cheating on her. When she added that she was overweight, I turned up the volume to listen more carefully. She then calmly told the host that with each extramarital affair, her eating had increased. In fact, she announced, her husband's cheating was totally her fault.

Having been a guest on this show myself, I knew some of the host's biases. So I wasn't surprised to hear him say, "When it comes to who's to blame in this situation, this woman is sure being honest." In essence, the host was holding the woman with the food addiction responsible for her husband's inappropriate sexual behavior. Turning down the volume, I shook my head sadly and made my way home.

In reality, the woman was responsible only for her food addiction. But she was convinced she deserved this sort of disrespectful treatment because of her weight. I wanted to say to her, "News flash! Your food addiction did *not* force your husband to have sex with other women! If he was so unhappy with you he could have sought out help for himself, divorced you, or talked to professionals about how your food addiction impacted the relationship!" By taking responsibility for his sexual acting out, this woman could continue to avoid coming to terms with the deep hurt, anger, shame, loneliness, and sense of betrayal she carried about her husband's many infidelities.

In denying these emotions and not holding her husband accountable for his addictive behavior, she not only had an excuse to eat compulsively, she was enabling him to continue acting out sexually. Her husband wasn't responsible for her food addiction, but he was accountable for his own addiction and the emotional hurt he was inflicting upon his wife. As long as the two addictions kept playing off one another, neither the wife nor the husband needed to take responsibility. Instead, they could continue to live in fantasyland. "I'm not perfect, so he has a right to cheat on me, which gives me the right to eat more." "She's not perfect, so I have the right to seek out perfect-looking fantasy women to sleep with." These are the myths these two were living by. Though this may sound like an extreme example, in actuality this couple wasn't all that unusual.

Sex and food are necessary for the continuation of our species. Without lust and an appetite, none of us would be here. Both sex and food can also be very pleasurable, but if we use them in an addictive manner, we distort our reality. Used compulsively, both food and sex have the capacity to change the way we feel about ourselves and the world around us. And the consequences of food or sex addiction can be as devastating as alcoholism or drug dependency.

Food and sex addictions cloud healthy intimacy, leaving many of us with inaccurate perceptions about ourselves and our relationships. Sex and intimacy aren't the same thing, but many of us have listened to pop culture and believe otherwise. Myths about sexually appropriate versus inappropriate behavior are always at the core of adult intimacy issues. We confuse love with sex, and our relationships suffer. Because of this, sexual addictions and eating addictions typically go hand in hand. On the sexual side, dysfunction, inappropriate acting out, affairs, excessive demands for sex or a lack of sex in a relationship are common. On the food side, compulsive eating, yo-yo dieting, self-starvation, or bingeing and purging may interact with those dysfunctions. It's important to recognize that food and sex addictions are dysfunctional survival skills that can play off one another, and that this pattern can destroy current and potential relationships. If a relationship has any chance of survival, it is essential to understand that:

- We may be using our partner's addiction as an excuse to not take responsibility for our own addictions and unresolved issues.

- When we do this, we hurt ourselves and continue to provide our current or future partners with excuses for acting out addictively.

- When we enable dysfunction in others, our relationships don't have a chance.

Removing the foggy rose-colored glasses of addiction forces us to finally see our relationships for what they are. Once our vision is clear, we need to be willing not only to take responsibility for our own healing, but to recognize that we just might be enabling our partners to stay lost in their own addictions. When we take steps to recover from these patterns, loving, healthy relationships can happen.

• • •

9

Are Kids the Problem? Or Are They Being Used As a Barrier to Intimacy?

Mom and Pop were just a couple of kids when they got married.
He was eighteen, she was sixteen, and I was three.

— BILLIE HOLIDAY, JAZZ SINGER AND SONGWRITER

One rainy morning, my son Aaron showed up on my doorstep. On the spur of the moment, he'd decided to come home from college for a brief visit. After he put down a tennis bag stuffed full of dirty laundry, I gave my handsome firstborn a big hug and asked him if he was hungry. Being so happy to see him, I didn't even complain about the stinky tennis shoes and socks in need of a good soak. Thankfully, I hadn't scheduled any clients until that afternoon, so as the washing machine spun and rinsed, Aaron and I spent the rest of the morning catching up. Listening to him share his excitement about going into teaching, I felt a deep sense of gratitude and drew in a sigh of relief. It was good to see him so happy.

Most of us want what's best for our children. We want them to be prepared to leave the predictable, secure nest of home and to successfully make it in a world full of uncertainty. For some time, my son had struggled to decide on a college major. Feeling lost in an overwhelming university setting, Aaron had floundered terribly for the first year. Seeing him so energetic and pleased with the path he had finally chosen, I was relieved that he had survived his months of confusion and emotional

131

distress. Aaron had left the safety of our family, gone off to begin a new chapter of his life, hit a few brick walls, and then successfully navigated around them.

Being a parent is one of the most difficult jobs on the planet, but when a child is born no one hands us an instruction manual. My own mother was diagnosed with cancer when I was an impressionable twelve-year old. Shortly after I turned sixteen she died a tragic, painful death. She was just thirty-eight. Before the cancer, my turbulent childhood had rotated around the substance abuse of both my parents. My mother and father were two deeply wounded souls in need of much healing. Because of drugs and alcohol, neither was emotionally equipped to raise children. Holding Aaron in my arms right after he was born, I knew my ability to be a healthy parent was never going to come from the parenting I had received as a child.

Michael, my husband, came from a family that gave him everything he ever wanted. He was truly a spoiled child. His parents rarely, if ever, set any limits or boundaries with him, and he was the center of their universe. (That remained true even at the age of forty!) Michael had a credit card and a car by the time he was fourteen, he spent his summers in France, and went to a private high school in Aspen, the playland of the rich and famous. Neither of his parents ever had a great deal of money, but they were willing to go into debt for their children. Both parents were immigrants who had suffered many losses during the Holocaust. Wanting to be good parents, they "overdid" for their children and over-empowered them. As a result, Michael experienced very little frustration or disappointment during his childhood. He grew into a young man who thought he could rescue a destructive, alcoholic, drug-addicted wife, and, married to me, was confronted for the first time with frustration and disappointment. Because of his upbringing he didn't have the life skills to navigate such treacherous waters at first.

Thankfully, we didn't have children until after I sobered up and had tackled a few issues I had about my own chaotic upbringing. When we eventually did have a child, we discovered that because we had such different backgrounds, we also had very opposing ideas about parenting.

This conflict forced us to take a good, hard look at ourselves. Each of us knew that to be effective, balanced, healthy parents, we had more individual healing to do. Our graduate degrees in psychology hadn't solved any of our issues, and my sobriety had brought more unhealthy patterns to the surface of my awareness. Both of us still had childhood history that, if left unaddressed, could have tainted our ability to parent our son. Michael was at risk for not setting any boundaries, rescuing, and overdoing for our children, while I was fearful I'd be too rigid in my parenting. And because there was so much violence in my family, I had the potential to be an overprotective mother not only with Aaron, but with his younger brother Joshua too.

After healing individually, we also needed to clean up some pretty hefty concerns that for years had loomed over our marriage. Addressing our addictions, resentments, and poor communication skills finally fostered healthy intimacy between us, enabling us to be emotionally present parents. If we had not done this work, we would have been in jeopardy of using both of our children as buffers with each other and as distractions from our own unresolved painful emotions.

Looking over my cup of coffee at my oldest son, I knew Aaron was going to be all right. Michael and I had done what we needed to do to explore and resolve our own early losses. Our childhood issues hadn't clouded our ability to be the parents Aaron had needed for us to be. His father and I had prepared him well for adulthood by providing him with the life skills he would need to handle difficult times.

After lunch with Aaron, I went to the office to see a few clients. Walking into the waiting room, I saw a multitude of toys scattered everywhere, all pulled from the shelves where they were kept for child clients and visitors. In the mix of plastic dinosaurs, building blocks, colored pencils, and stuffed animals was a half-eaten hamburger, a few squashed french fries, and a partially consumed, melting chocolate milkshake. Before I could take in the whole scene, one of my office partners entered and made a beeline for me. She was not in a good mood. As she stepped over an empty fast food bag, I saw she was holding pieces of a ceramic figurine in her hands. "Carla," she sighed, "I hate to do this, but you are going to have to pay for this."

Looking carefully at the fragile pieces, I noticed they had once been part of a pretty ballerina who was now missing her nose, an arm, and a leg. Before I could say "I'm sorry" I heard a loud *meow!* Turning toward the door of my office, I spotted one of my young clients. Sammy was nine years old with rusty red hair and a devilish grin. Clutched tightly in his arms was the office cat, which lived outside on the front porch. The poor elderly orange tabby had adopted us some years back. After a few dishes of cat food he had decided to call the porch home.

"Sammy?" I asked. "Why were you outside? You know the rules. No leaving the building, and no playing with Tom the cat! Please put Tom down!" Sammy didn't put the cat down but instead took him into my office. Following him, I saw that the carnage in the waiting room was minimal compared to what was waiting for me in my office. Sammy's younger sister Jenny had taken every toy she could find from the shelves, while their mother Melinda sat on the couch talking on her cell phone. Jenny had red hair just like her brother, and as I walked in she cheerfully tossed back her curls and said, "Hi! Wanna see what I can do with this car?" Before I could answer no, she was running the blue Mustang up my leg. Turning to the couch, I was about to ask Melinda to give me a hand, but she quickly raised one finger, signaling she would be off of her phone soon.

In the joy of seeing my son, I had completely forgotten that this session with this particular mom and her children was going to be my first case for the day. Typically, I made it a point to be in the office before they arrived.

Looking around me, I decided, "No use crying over spilt milk or chocolate milkshakes." It was time to clean things up. Sammy had dropped Tom, and the cowering kitty was desperately trying to hide behind my desk. After scooping him up, I turned to Sammy and said, "I'm going to give you three things to do. First, pick up all of the toys in the waiting room. Second, throw all of your uneaten food and the wrappers in the trash can. And third, you will need to apologize to my office partner for breaking her ballerina. She's feeling very sad."

My usual reward for Sammy was a short walk to the park down the street to play on the swings, so I added, "If you do not do these three things, we will not be able to play at the park today." As Sammy slowly began picking up his mess, I put Tom outside, walked back into my office and said to his sister Jenny, "And, if you want to go to the park, you too have some work to do. Put these toys back where they belong." Heaving a great sigh, she replied, "Okay."

Before these two children first began visiting my office, no boundaries had ever been set with them. They did as they pleased and rarely took responsibility for their actions. Both had been diagnosed with attention-deficit/hyperactivity disorder (ADHD) and were on medications. Having worked with kids with disabilities over the years, I had concerns that their mother Melinda not only catered to Sammy and Jenny because of their disabilities, but that she organized too much of her life around them. Because their diagnosis was the center of her world, she expected everyone else to tolerate their unacceptable behavior. As a result, both children were having problems at school.

Melinda finally hung up her cell phone. "That was the school. Sammy got in trouble again! I swear they refuse to understand what it is I'm dealing with!" Angrily she threw the phone on the couch, got on her knees next to Jenny, and started hastily picking up toys. I had always believed that both Sammy and Jenny had attention difficulties, but I wasn't convinced it was true ADHD. They had little if any structure in their lives, and both of them knew how to manipulate their mother. Because Sammy and Jenny rarely had limits set at home, they carried these expectations into school. When their teachers set limits, this initially intensified the inappropriate behavior.

When Melinda called the school to rescue her children from the consequences of their behavior, she only made matters worse. The lesson they learned was, "We can do what we want and Mom will fix it." The structured classroom experience would eventually prove helpful, and both children would begin to improve in their schoolwork and conduct. Sadly, Melinda wasn't always good about setting consistent limits and keeping a schedule at home. When she faltered, again it was back to square one. The school psychologist had offered Melinda plenty of suggestions and support for coping and assisting her children, but she rarely took it. Melinda's identity centered on being the mother of two children with diagnosed disabilities.

She and the children's father were divorced, and after several other failed relationships, Melinda was now dating again. She continued to believe that if she found the right man, one who could accept her children, her problems would be solved. All of the men she had been involved with had been emotionally unavailable. It was only a matter of time before she figured out that the latest man in her life had a substance abuse problem. She had mentioned to me in passing that her lawyer boyfriend smoked marijuana daily, but then quickly added, "At least he isn't a drunk like all of the rest!" Instead of looking at this pattern of hers, Melinda was convinced that her relationships didn't work out because her partners didn't understand her commitment to her children.

Melinda's ex-husband, Robert, had eventually sobered up and was regularly attending Alcoholics Anonymous. I suggested to Melinda that she investigate Al-Anon, a Twelve Step program for the friends and family members of alcoholics, but she had said, "I don't have time for that. With these two kids? Are you crazy? When am I going to find the time to go to meetings? Maybe if Robert didn't go to so many meetings, then I could go to meetings!"

As a divorced couple, Robert and Melinda had a lot of unfinished business to address. When they came to therapy together, they spent most of their time attacking one another on parenting issues. Their unresolved hidden resentments continually pushed aside any discussion about the structure and consistency needed for both Sammy and Jenny. Robert blamed Melinda for the unhappiness in his life, and Melinda was convinced that if it hadn't been for Robert she would be in a much better place. That was as far as their discussion had gone about their failed marriage.

Both parents had been talking negatively about each other to the children, which was escalating their acting-out behavior at school. Their toxic resentment toward one another was distracting them from healthy parenting, so I had to switch gears. Before they could work together as a team, these parents had to start addressing their unresolved history with each other. We were making some progress. Each of them was making a list of what they disliked about their ex-partner, and later they would read these lists out loud during a joint marital session.

Now, shaking my head, I said, "If Robert doesn't go to meetings, he will be a risk for drinking again. And you need to go to meetings because you keep dating men with addiction problems." Melinda was not convinced. She asked again, "Well, who's going to look after the children while we are both hob-nobbing at these meetings? And who will deal with the phone calls I've been getting from the school about the children? Not Robert!"

Melinda was a master at deflecting attention from herself to her children, but this time it wasn't going to work. "Melinda, you need to let your children suffer some natural consequences. Children with academic, emotional, or physical disabilities get in trouble just like other kids do. If you keep doing everything for them, cleaning up messes they should be taking care of themselves, arguing with the school each time teachers set limits, and rotating your life around their diagnoses, you will never focus in on your own issues and the children will never learn to be responsible for their actions."

As Melinda shoved plastic blocks into a bag, she turned and with controlled rage said, "What do you know? I was totally on my own as a child, and I was utterly responsible. I was the perfect child. My parents never even knew I had problems. We were the picture-perfect family who never talked about anything that even suggested heartache, anger, hurt, rage, or pain. If I was upset about something, like a neighbor kid reaching under my skirt and touching me where he wasn't supposed to, I just tucked it away and acted as if it never happened. I knew I couldn't tell my parents about my problems, because we just didn't talk about such things. I will never do that to my children. I will always be here for them, no matter what, and I will never abandon them the way my parents abandoned me." I knew that Melinda and I had plenty more to talk about.

After cleaning up my office, Melinda moved to go out into the waiting room to gather up Sammy's clutter. He had decided to not pick up the piles of toys and food products he had strewn around the room and had been crying out for her to help him. "I can't do it by myself! It's not fair!" I heard him sob. "Melinda?" I asked. "Why don't you try not rescuing him? Just humor me. Sit on the couch for just a few minutes before you go out into the waiting room." Melinda plopped herself unwillingly onto the couch, and her son begin to wail.

Looking at Jenny, I smiled and asked, "What do you think? Is that fake crying or real crying?" Grinning, she said, "Real fake crying!" We both chuckled and then I said, "You knew your mommy would clean up the office for you, didn't you? Would you have done a little fake crying if she hadn't?" As Jenny played with a teddy bear, she smiled again and said, "Probably." Getting on the floor with her, I asked, "Well, how are you ever going to learn how to pick up after yourself if your mommy is always doing it?" In all seriousness, she looked me straight in the eye and answered, "My mommy will always be there to pick up for me forever!" Glancing up at Melinda on the couch, I noticed she looked a bit surprised by what Jenny had just said.

What Happens in Dysfunctional Families

If a couple brings a child to my office for a consult, I always ask the adults what's going on with them. Specifically, I ask them how their own relationship is going. In my profession, it is a well-known fact that when parents or caretakers have difficulties in their personal lives or with one another, their children are at risk for acting out the associated emotions and stresses. Even if adult problems are hidden, children will still feel the tension in the family related to these unaddressed emotions. In turn, couples with intimacy disorders, relationship difficulties, or unresolved issues of their own will often distract themselves by focusing on the behavior of their children.

How often I've heard clients use their children's acting-out behavior as an excuse to not go to therapy, treatment, or support group meetings themselves. "How can I leave my child for a workshop on intimacy when my son is having such a rough time? Besides, his father is the one with the problem. Not me!" These parents or caregivers may tend to organize every free second of their lives around a child's diagnosis—for example, ADD (or the related ADHD, attention-deficit hyperactivity disorder) or other learning disability. The diagnosis gives them a sense of identity and becomes an excuse to not practice self-care. Instead of understanding, "Geez, I'm upset over the divorce, death of a parent or child, alcoholism, job loss, or unresolved sexual abuse I experienced as a child," these parents will focus a narrow spotlight of constant worry onto a child's acting-out behavior.

Over-parenting has also become a modern norm. Society reinforces this behavior by telling us we are good parents when we overdo for our kids. But hiding from our relationship issues behind socially acceptable excessive parenting isn't fair to us or to our children. Society also tends to feel sorry for us when we have problem children, and this can encourage our distraction. Moreover, as a by-product of this trend, I believe we currently overdiagnose and overmedicate children with ADHD and other conditions. As parents, many of us are pressured into sacrificing ourselves for our children's welfare with excessive medication regimens and professional visits, too many behavioral programs and adjunct school activities. As long as we are so overly focused on our children, we won't have time to examine our own lives. And if we don't take care of our needs. our children will act out. It's a continuous cycle that never seems to end.

Relationship hopping isn't healthy for parents or kids either. Parents addicted to the chase, moving from one relationship to the next, often feel guilty about such behavior, which in turn affects parenting. Instead of setting appropriate limits with kids, these parents may instead give in to their demands. Such children can grow into adolescents without boundaries who have difficulty hearing the word no. This in turn creates problems at home and school. When this occurs, parents again have one more reason to ignore their own issues and attend only to their acting-out teenagers. Other parents, feeling guilty about a divorce or the time they've spent addictively chasing romance, try to compensate by overindulging youngsters materially. Overdoing, over-giving, and not setting appropriate limits with kids creates future adults who can be self-centered, self absorbed, and addicted to immediate gratification. They will also be at risk for empty, addictive relationships in adulthood.

With the high divorce rate in our country, we are setting the stage for our own children to not understand what a healthy partnership with another person looks like. We are unknowingly creating generations of adults who haven't learned how to hash out relationship problems. Because so many of us have modeled unhealthy relationship behavior, this responsibility lies with us. Unfortunately, many of us parents never had good models either, because our own parents never healed from their own dysfunction and intimacy issues. We must heal. Without healing, the addictive quality of the lustful chase will displace the real ingredients for a successful relationship, and we will be at risk for passing this message on to our children.

Most parents don't like to hear that they might be using their children as a distraction to their own life difficulties. But most parents I work with are unaware that their unaddressed intimacy issues are impacting the children they love and cherish.

Intimacy Barriers, Real Issues, and Confusion

Years ago I worked with a family with several children one of whom was challenged with mental retardation. The mother, a war veteran, had been injured in battle. In addition to her injury, she came home with post-traumatic stress disorder (PTSD), a psychological condition that follows a traumatic event, often with symptoms occurring long afterward. PTSD not only disrupts the person's life, it has been scientifically shown to impact every member of the sufferer's family, including the children. Such was the case for this family.

The mother had a very long healing process that consumed her both physically and emotionally. At the same time, the six-year-old mentally challenged son, whose home and school routines had been working well, began acting out. Both parents now focused closely on the child's negative behavior. With this excessive attention, the boy's difficulties only increased, and as his behavior escalated his parents focused even more on him.

Why did this happen? With Mom's return home, the balance and routines in the family were disrupted. In addition, the couple had some unaddressed relationship issues that were causing tension. The mother wouldn't talk about her war experiences with her husband and started to pull away, which created even more tension. Instead of addressing any of these difficult concerns, both parents focused more of their attention on their mentally challenged child.

By the time they reached my office, the couple had not been sexual for over a year, and the father was on the verge of an affair. Both of them were consuming more alcohol, and the mother was on several medications for anxiety. After they presented their concerns about their son, I asked my usual question, "And what about your own relationship?" As the couple began to resolve some of their difficulties, losses, and traumas, balance returned to the home and the mentally challenged son, along with two other older sisters, settled down.

Using our kids to distract us from our own unresolvedintimacy issues doesn't serve them or us. If we are in a relationship, those issues will eventually create distance between us and our partner. Living with loneliness in a relationship hurts us and our kids, and in many cases it can set us up to seek out a mood-altering new relationship. If we are single parents, our children can become an excuse for not confronting intimacy issues. We may date but have difficulty with commitment, or we may find ourselves with partners who are unable to commit. Believing that most of our time must be devoted to our children, we don't take time to heal ourselves. This isn't good for parents or kids.

Children are emotional sponges. Young kids and even teenagers can feel responsible for the emotions their parents are feeling. Children know when something is wrong. Unfortunately they don't have the maturity to understand that whatever's going on with mom or dad may have nothing to do with them. Feeling responsible, they can feel burdened with the stress associated with their parents' intimacy issues. I remember acting out as a child when both of my divorced parents were addictively moving from one relationship to the next. In such situations, anxiety begins to build and overwhelm children, and eventually they act out to discharge the emotion. Once they do, their behavior becomes a focus for parents who should be looking at their own dysfunctions. It's a vicious cycle and nobody wins.

How Functional Families Deal with Stress

In healthy families, acting-out behavior can be related to problems at school, difficulty with classmates, stress between siblings, physical illness, growth spurts or hormonal changes, the loss of a loved one or pet, upset over limits imposed at home or school, or a true emotional disability or learning disorder. In healthy families acting out can also be related to temporary relationship difficulties between parents.

In healthy family systems, the following standards apply, even during times of stress:

- There is flexibility regarding roles and rules, but parents are able to take control in healthy ways.

- Parents can communicate expectations in a productive, useful, non-shaming, and healthy manner.

- All family members are encouraged to take responsibility for their own feelings, behaviors, and attitudes.

- All family members are taught to respect each other, and all members' needs are recognized.

- The family can adapt to change or deal with crisis in a healthy manner.

- Family members are encouraged to develop the ability to listen and to empathize with each other and others.

- There is a sense of trust, unity, and belonging for each member of the system.

- Family members are encouraged to have their own identities, and individual boundaries are respected.

- Parents have a life of their own away from the children.

- Family members have a sense of humor and the ability to laugh with one another.

- All members of the family are able to grow and learn.

A variety of factors can create imbalance in a family: stress and change, chaotic schedules, disagreements, infidelity, unemployment, illness or death, or any other type of loss or upset. All relationships have problems. If parents properly address and resolve their issues, children won't absorb the unhealthy emotions associated with them. How parents cope with difficult situations sets the stage for how children react and how long the imbalance will persist. In healthy families, there might be temporary swings in behavior from one extreme to another, but eventually balance returns.

What's a Parent to Do?

How can you make sure you are taking care of your relationship and being the best parent possible? Always take time for yourself. If you are sacrificing your needs for your children's wants, giving up your therapy time to carpool kids to one more activity, you are out of balance. Get back into balance. Take a look at your own over-parenting behavior and ask yourself how it keeps you from attending to your needs and relationships. If you are confused about what healthy parenting looks like, visit with a licensed child psychologist to get some information. Then honestly look at your intimate relationships to see if you've been hiding from unresolved issues by over-parenting.

If you are divorced or single and find yourself feeling guilty for dating, and being away from your children, you probably need to sit down and ask yourself why. Are your children used to having all of your time and attention? Until now, have you been over-parenting to avoid taking risks and committing to relationships or exploring dating more fully? Do you need to seek out a family therapist to learn how to talk with your children about dating? Or has the emotional high of the chase kept you from being the parent you need to be? Are your children now acting out to get your attention?

If you're in a committed partnership, when you feel tension in your relationship, don't ignore it by overengaging in kid-related activities: school projects or PTA, piano practice, baseball. (And don't overindulge your kiddos materially, either.) Never expect your kids to emotionally fill up the emptiness you might be feeling in your primary relationship. I've worked with too many clients who have resigned from the role of parent in order to become their child's "friend." This often happens when there is loneliness in the primary relationship—typically a by-product of unresolved, perhaps unspoken intimacy issues. As the emotional gap between parents widens, children are often expected to fill it with friendship relationships with parents. We can't expect our kids to fill that role. It's not their job. Using our children as buffers harms everyone involved. If you are feeling lonely in your relationship, grab your partner and take the time needed to sort out your differences. If you can't do this on your own, visit with a marriage and family therapist.

If you don't know how to have healthy intimacy with yourself or a partner, don't do what so many of our parents did. Don't blame it on the kids. Instead of denying there's a problem, admit to yourself you are in trouble. Honestly take responsibility for your own life, past history, current difficulties, and relationships. Face up to your relationship issues, your anger over the death of a relationship or love affair, and your grief over dreams that never panned out. And then go get some help! Then, when you focus on your children's needs and wants, you will be doing so for all the right reasons.

As parents, we are never failures just because we make mistakes. We only fail as parents when we neglect to rectify those mistakes. By taking care of all of our adult needs we are being good parents. When we do this, we are modeling healthy self-care and life skills for navigating the rough waters of adulthood. What better gift can we give our children?

• • •

10

Using Religion as a Cover: Hiding from Healthy Intimacy

I have sinned against you, and I beg your forgiveness.

— REV. JIMMY SWAGGART, APOLOGIZING TO HIS WIFE IN A TELEVISED SERMON
AFTER BEING CAUGHT WITH A PROSTITUTE

Adam turned to his wife of twenty years and pleaded, "It's just a box of porno. I don't know why you're so upset. It's not like I'm spending my time going through these magazines every day!" Adam was a good-looking middle-aged man who taught high school math and was the youth director at his church. Looking at me for support he said, "The way she talks, you'd think I was hanging around strip clubs and picking up prostitutes like my dad!" Turning back to his wife, Adam asked, "If God forgives me, why can't you?" Georgia was doing her best to control her emotions, but I could tell she was having a hard time. Her irritation was beginning to show as she said to her husband, "That's exactly what you said when I discovered you were having an affair with a congregant from our church! You said God had forgiven you and I should too. You even used biblical scripture to try to convince me that I was out of line for feeling so betrayed."

As her husband continued to make excuses for both the pornography and the affair, Georgia became stoic and silent. The woman radiated all the qualities of a Southern Belle. Every article of her clothing matched perfectly, right down to the flowered tennis shoes with colored laces.

Though the prim and proper appearance was convincing, behind the controlled church-lady facade was a mind sharp as a tack. Aside from being the devoted mother of two teenage daughters, Georgia had a Ph.D. in divinity and was also one of the lead ministers at the church the family attended.

Michael and I had been seeing the couple in therapy for about a month, and the extramarital affair was new information for both of us. Originally, the entire family had been referred to me by a clergy friend of mine. The older daughter had spent a night in jail after receiving a DWI. Her excessive drinking and drug use had taken both of her parents totally by surprise. After they successfully intervened on the chemically dependent teen for inpatient treatment, unresolved issues were now surfacing for both Adam and Georgia.

Because Georgia had revealed Adam's past indiscretion to us, I could tell he was feeling embarrassed, so I asked, "How long ago was the affair?" Sheepishly, Adam replied, "Fifteen years ago, and it was the only one! My father, who's a preacher, still cheats on my mother, and he's in his seventies." With this revelation, Michael said, "Did you know people who cheat often come from families where parents or even grandparents were unfaithful to their primary relationships?" Georgia's anger was rising as she said, "His father's affairs were a secret until just a few years ago. Up until that point everyone in town thought he walked on water, so how could that have affected Adam? That excuse won't fly with me. Even his mother didn't know."

Michael glanced over at me, so I took the lead and said, "Well, most people don't realize that even when affairs or addictions are kept secret from a partner, the feelings associated with these behaviors don't just evaporate into thin air." Looking at Adam, I continued, "Your mother may not have consciously known about the extramarital affairs, but most likely she knew intuitively something wasn't right. She felt your father distancing from her and most likely blamed herself for this." Now Georgia appeared to have a new awareness. Turning to Adam, she said, "I felt like that when you were having your affair. I always thought you were mad at me or upset with something I'd done, even when you told me that wasn't the case. Adam, I felt you pull away from me." Adam looked very surprised.

To see Georgia relating this way showed great progress, so I kept on educating. "People who act out with compulsive behaviors or addiction, like your daughter did with drugs and alcohol, do so to escape feeling." Seeing Adam was confused, I added, "Adam, you and your father have used sex to mask your emotions." Looking at both of them, I said, "Being preoccupied or having an obsession of any sort can numb us from feeling anger, fear, loneliness, hurt, stress, sadness, shame, and insecurity. Though this may work for a while, the price we pay for temporarily feeling numb eventually catches up with us. When obsession and addiction are present, healthy, honest communication can't take place. Over time, intimacy with those we love begins to die because these preoccupations are not only mentally consuming but based on secrecy and dishonesty."

As I continued, I noticed Adam wasn't looking nearly as defensive as he had during the first few minutes of the session. "For example," I continued, "if I'm really upset about a death in my family and don't know how to grieve, I'm going to start feeling really uncomfortable in my own skin. After awhile that constant sense of anxiety will build and feel overwhelming. In response to this, maybe I'll go eat a cake, gamble my paycheck away, drink a few beers, overspend on the credit card, pop a couple of extra sleeping pills, watch soap operas, spend hours at the computer, become engrossed with a project at work, fantasize about a good-looking guy at the office, or zone out with a porno magazine. One way or another, I'm going to find some way to distance myself from my feelings of grief. Unfortunately, aside from distancing from my grief, I'll also be distancing from those I love. I'll never heal my feelings of loss, and in the future I'll be more likely to use addiction or obsession to avoid dealing with life's challenges. Every once in a while we all need to escape emotionally, but if we're doing so on a regular basis, this can turn into a living problem."

Looking at Georgia, I added, "Your parents have used alcohol to run from their life difficulties for years. And the anger I saw on your face when you shared this tells me their addiction directly impacts you too." Tears welled up in her eyes, but she quickly regained control and said, "Yes, and if it weren't for my religion I don't know where I'd be. My church gave me the surrogate family I so desperately needed during my youth. If it hadn't been for my religious community, who knows what would have happened to me." Turning to Adam, I said, "It looks like your father has used extramarital affairs to avoid dealing with his feelings. What complicates this even more is that he's covered up his shame about cheating with religion."

Glaring at me, Georgia asked, "Are you attacking religion? I just told you religion kept me sane through my own parents' alcoholism and that my faith helped me survive Adam's affair. The only reason we as a family came to see you is because we were referred your way by a minister friend who does therapy himself." Seeing how upset Georgia was, Michael quickly took over to defuse the situation. "Yes, religion is a wonderful thing. Faith is an essential ingredient in the lives of people all around the world, but sometimes religion can be misused as a cover for some pretty serious problems."

Seeing that Georgia was still angry, Michael asked Adam, "What did you two do as a couple to resolve the hurt feelings related to your affair?" After glancing at Georgia, he replied, "Well, she didn't speak to me for months. No one at church knew about it because the woman I had the affair with stopped coming to services. I started reading the Bible daily, and I talked to one of the other ministers about it. He said I needed to pray and ask for forgiveness, so I did. For some time I felt really bad, but after a while the whole episode sort of took a backseat to more serious troubles." The sun was setting, so I got up to close the blinds. Afterward, I sat back down and asked Georgia, "What problems is he talking about?"

Now in full control of her emotions, Georgia briskly brushed some lint off her skirt and replied, "Around the time of his affair, I'd had three miscarriages. For some reason I couldn't stay pregnant. I guess it just wasn't God's will. There was even a part of me that thought God was punishing me." Surprised, I asked her, "Why would God punish you?"

Looking uncomfortable, she continued. "At that point I was also very angry with my father. Along with his drinking, he was hitting the casino and putting himself and my mother into debt. They came to me for a loan and I said no. We were barely getting by ourselves, and I just didn't have money to spare. Adam was finishing up college and I'd just started working as an assistant minister where the pay was almost nothing."

Finally, the situation was beginning to make sense. Looking at Michael, I could tell he was also putting two and two together. "That must have been incredibly painful for the both of you," he said. "Miscarriages are a grief issue. They're nature's way of saying physically something isn't right, but do you really believe God was punishing you? Do you really think it's your job to take care of your parents when they're perfectly capable of taking care of themselves? If our loved ones are behaving irresponsibly because of an addiction and we rescue them when they get into trouble, we're actually not helping matters. Instead, we're adding to the problem. They'll never figure out that their addictions are creating their trials and tribulations if we keep rescuing them." Georgia was finally letting a few tears fall. I then asked, "What did your parents do when you said no?" Wiping her eyes she responded, "They took out a second mortgage on the house and stopped speaking to me."

I could tell these two had a lot of work to do. "So, at the beginning of your relationship you had financial hardships, major losses, and difficult parents to deal with," I summarized. "Georgia, you were focusing in on your new career. The intensity and stress of a new job demanded your attention. Adult children of alcoholics or any type of dysfunction are often very good at edging out painful life concerns with a particular project, task, or career. This is how many of us block out the insanity of our younger years. Yes, your faith did provide you with an island of sanity during some really rough times. Sadly, you also used religion in a very negative manner to explain the miscarriages. Because you didn't give your alcoholic father money, you decided the miscarriages were your punishment."

"Believing God was punishing you enabled you to blame yourself for the miscarriages. In doing this you didn't have to look at the stresses you were under. The majority of these stresses were out of your control, but in blaming yourself you were able to hold on to the illusion of being in control. Most adult children of alcoholics have a hard time feeling out of control. It feels like death! The belief is, 'I should be able to handle all of this by myself! If I can't, I'm a failure or a bad person!' You didn't have miscarriages because you were a bad person. These tragic losses weren't your fault." Georgia was silently weeping and nodding in agreement, so I turned to Adam.

"Adam, you escaped the pain of loss by reenacting the dysfunction you sensed in your home as a young boy. Though you may not have consciously known about your father's extramarital affairs, a part of you felt the tension in your family. Because your father was living two very different lives, the confusion must have been overwhelming for you. On the one hand, he was the pillar of the community, preaching about morality every Sunday. People most likely believed you were lucky to have such a 'wonderful' father. At the same time, there was this secretive, preoccupied, and obsessed side to him. The affairs were his unconscious solution for distancing himself from the issues and emotions he didn't know how to address. This dark side also put distance between you and him."

As I talked, Adam was agreeing, and I could tell he was feeling sad. "For you, the feelings of emotional remoteness and isolation in your family eventually turned to loneliness for you. Loneliness can set up sexual acting out. Having never received the skills necessary for connecting with others on an emotionally safe, open, honest, and intimate level, sex was used to temporarily fill up that feeling of isolation. So, instead of talking to Georgia about your sense of loss over the miscarriages, you turned to an affair to run from your feelings, just as your father did." Both Adam and Georgia were listening without interrupting, but I could tell Michael had something to say, so I stopped there.

"During our previous sessions together these serious relationship issues never came up," Michael pointed out. "I suspect you didn't even know you were supposed to talk about them, but I'm glad they've finally surfaced. Up until now what we did know was that you both spent a lot of time at church and your lives rotated around your religious community." Looking at Adam, he continued, "Like your father, you and your wife are the pillars of your religious community, and your congregation believes you're the perfect family. So have you told anyone at your church that your daughter is in treatment for substance abuse?" Concerned, Georgia asked, "As a minister, how can I tell the people who depend on me that I'm having problems?" Adam quickly added, "I suppose you think we should tell everyone about my affair too? That will ruin me as a church youth director!"

Seeing how fearful both of them were, I quickly said, "Hiding your pain behind religion and religious duties—hiding it from those who care about you—is really inappropriate and unhealthy. A truly spiritual person understands that community supports personal intimacy and a sense of connectedness. Everyone has problems, and all of us need good friends who'll allow us to be vulnerable when we are down. So in answer to your question, no, you don't need to tell your congregation everything about your lives, but you do need a few close friends. Do either of you have any supports for yourselves?"

Georgia and Adam blankly stared first at one another and then at us. Finally Georgia spoke, "Our church community would do anything for us, but no. We provide the shoulders for people to cry on. I thought I could just turn to God and my Bible by myself, but I guess I need more. Scripture is so comforting, but yes, I'd love to learn how to trust a few people with my problems. Our daughter's drug addiction nearly did me in. It's been so refreshing to sit in family group at the treatment center every week and really talk about how I feel. Adam won't share his feelings because he's afraid it'll get back to our congregation. For me, every time I've opened my mouth, I've felt such relief! If only I'd had this kind of support after I found out Adam was having an affair." The tears were returning as she added, "I'm still so hurt about that and now . . . the pornography?" Her voice trailed off.

Upset again, Adam interjected, "Wasn't I told by a minister that in the eyes of God I was forgiven? I made a mistake and had one short affair. It was stupid! Why do you keep bringing it up? It happened years ago. Can't you let it go? Isn't that what you tell your congregation to do?" With these words, Georgia began to cry hard. The caretaking minister front had finally given way to a wounded woman at her wits' end.

As the flow of tears began to subside, Michael handed Georgia a box of tissues and said, "It must be exhausting to always feel you have to be so in control of your emotions. You offer people spiritual reassurance daily, while you yourself are on empty. You wouldn't expect members of your congregation to go off alone with their secrets and troubles, with just a Bible and no support. No, you're there for them. You hold their hands while they prayed and even cried. Why shouldn't you receive the same sort of connected nourishment? Your expectations of yourself are so high." Hearing these words, Georgia started to cry again.

Now I told Adam, "If you and Georgia don't heal your individual and relationship issues, the unresolved emotions you have will continue to surface. Just ignoring your pain won't make it go away. Faith is wonderful if you follow it with action. Both of you have misused religion to bandage some very deep wounds. Why not use your religion as it was intended? According to your religious tradition there's a verse in the Bible that says 'Faith without works is dead.' You can try to pray away your difficulties, but if you don't take active responsibility in attempting to resolve your losses they will continue to follow you."

Adam nodded in agreement and said, "James 2:20. Now it makes sense. I can read the Bible all day long and continue to be stuck. It's sort of like wanting to learn how to parachute out of an airplane. I'd start by reading a book, but then I'd need some hands-on instruction in order to know how to open the chute and land without breaking my legs."

I was relieved to see that the points I'd been trying to get across for almost an hour were finally sinking in. Looking over at Michael, I smiled and he knew it was his turn to speak. "Adam, it's important for you to know that the pain your wife is feeling about the affair isn't just her problem. You need to look at why it happened in the first place. Also, instead of sharing how you were feeling about your daughter's chemical dependency, you started to slip back into sexual obsession with pornography. This too tells me you have work to do. You still have shame about your father the preacher and his extramarital affairs. This isn't healthy for you or your relationship."

"Georgia, your feelings about his affair are as strong as ever," Michael continued. "For years you've pushed these feeling under the rug and at times denied there's even a rug! You need to feel all of your feelings fully.This is the only way you'll be able to move them on out and forgive Adam. It'll take time, but this part of the relationship can be healed. Like Adam, you too have a lot of hidden feelings about your childhood and how your alcoholic parents have treated you as an adult. Both of you have family history that needs your attention. Attend to your feelings about this history, and the intimacy in your relationship will improve dramatically. Finally, if you both grieve the miscarriages together, say good-bye and really let go, the losses won't haunt you as badly as they do now."

Adam and Georgia looked relieved to have some direction. The session was over, so I slowly stood up. My poor skier's knees were feeling stiff. Smiling, I said, "You can have a healthy spiritual life if you make peace with yourselves as individuals. This in turn will enable you to experience more authentic intimacy in your relationship with one another. Once this happens, you'll be of better service to those who depend on you."

Religious Obsession: The Blanket Obsession

As we have seen, many of us unconsciously use specific obsessive behaviors to distance ourselves from our relationship issues. One of the most ignored forms of obsession has its roots in religion. Sometimes, dysfunctional partners misuse religious ideology and practices—including New Age approaches—to avoid looking at communication problems and even sexual matters. Because religion is used to mask such a wide a variety of issues, it can be seen as a "blanket obsession." Statements like these show us some examples:

- "God doesn't like it when we get angry and fight. So let's do God's will: no more disagreements."

- "Because I'm becoming more spiritually evolved, I don't worry about the credit card payments. The universe will provide, and you should trust me."

- "Yes, my mother sexually abused me, but the Bible says I must honor her. I should be a loving daughter and put the past in the past—no more conflict."

- "Every now and then I may drink too much, but getting angry over this won't help our relationship. Our meditation teacher said only love can cure our problems. You need to understand my stress."

- "I don't care if you hate sex. Our religion says it's your duty to me."

- "That opinion about equality in a relationship goes against church teaching, so I don't want to hear it. I'm the man of the house."

- "I know I was violent last night. I promise you I'll pray that behavior away."

- "Okay! I admit I've been abusing pain pills. I've sinned, but Jesus forgives me and you should too!"

- "I'm not very emotionally available, but a good chakra alignment from my healer will right my energy, and I believe this will take care of it, so quit nagging me about forgetting our anniversary."

- "We haven't had sex for nine months, and I know I have sexual problems from the sexual abuse I experienced as a child. My guru told me this crystal would heal me. Cancel the therapy session and be patient."

In the above real-life situations, inappropriate behavior or relationship difficulties were sidestepped, excused, or even justified by one or both partners with some form or misinterpretation of religion or spirituality. My favorite New Age excuse came from a woman who told me,

"He's so psychic he needs to drink a lot of alcohol, otherwise he'd be overwhelmed with psychic energy all the time." When religion or spiritual philosophies are used to cover up relationship problems, it's difficult to develop healthy, open, intimate connectedness with a partner.

Religion versus Spirituality

Religion and spirituality aren't the same. Religious institutions have been created by humankind. Religious traditions almost always have their origins in historical spiritual experiences, but the nuts-and-bolts structures of the institutions themselves don't involve mysticism or encounters with the supernatural. The daily operation of a religious organization involves specific tasks, rules, leadership, and regulations. The structure enables the institution to function, while the life practices promoted by religion can encourage spirituality to flourish. In other words, religion provides many of us with the foundation and discipline we need to develop ourselves as healthy spiritual beings. Used properly, religious tools can help us get through rough times and embrace our inner sense of spirituality.

True spirituality involves periods of growth, which can be challenging, confusing, and emotionally painful. At these times, spiritually evolving people may question their religious base or get angry with their concept of God, Higher Power, or universal spiritual principle. With a life crisis, painful loss, difficult challenge, or time of grief, questioning our beliefs is a normal, healthy, and healing. When we work through a difficult life experience, faith and spirituality can reach an even deeper level.

But religious obsession—rigidly following the guidelines of a belief system to the extreme—doesn't always equate to spiritual health. A person can be both "religious" and spiritually void at the same time. With religious obsession, there's an excessive attachment to a particular belief system. It may also involves misuse of its rules and regulations, its philosophical foundations, its disciplines and lifestyle suggestions. And often there's a self-imposed intolerance of those who walk a different path.

Instead of using a belief system for nurturing and self-growth, the person obsessed with religion distorts or misuses doctrine and lifestyle guidelines to hide from reality, to avoid confronting situations or experiences that cause confusion, pain, grief, anger, or fear. Regardless of the belief system, with this particular type of obsession, healthy spiritual progress is blocked and psychological damage can occur.

Hiding from Relationship and Family Troubles with Religion

Years ago a religiously devout Jewish family stayed with Michael, the boys, and me for several days at our home. We'd had Orthodox Jewish friends live with us in the past, so Michael and I both thought we knew how to make our guests comfortable. Though I believed we were fully prepared for this family, with hindsight I see that nothing could have readied us for the religious obsession we encountered.

The wife was a very spiritual person. She used her religious devotion to connect with her spiritual self, and this was lovely to observe. Her prayer rituals seemed intertwined with her being, and after her meditations a sense of serenity enveloped her. The same could not be said for her husband. He often chastised her for not measuring up to his expectations and berated her over the religious disciplining of their children. He appeared to rigidly go through his prayer rituals without receiving any spiritual nourishment. And he always had a strong need to debate with me about why I didn't observe my own Judaism as he did. This man was exhausting, and I soon found myself hiding from him in my own house!

One afternoon the wife and I were having a cup of tea when she announced, "He's suffocating me. I can't stand it. He emotionally degrades me in front of anyone and everyone, and he's incredibly critical of the children. My son tries so hard to be the perfect little boy for his father, but it's never good enough. Every time I attempt to talk to him about our problems or how unhappy I am, he throws our religion at me. His expectations of me and the kids are too much. Not only don't we measure up in his eyes, but in his opinion, we fail God daily." In fact, I'd been amazed at how well versed she and the children were with Judaism and religious scripture. I found it hard to believe any of them could be seen as religious failures.

Wiping tears from her eyes, she continued, "We're all actually frightened of him. I know you've seen how he treats us. I've had enough, and I'm leaving him." A few more tears fell. "He's taken something so beautiful and made it into a weapon. I can't stand it. Our religion isn't meant to be used as a method for controlling others, but he manipulates us day and night with scripture, ritual, and prayer. My poor children are learning to hate our religion, and he's destroyed our marriage with his brand of warped spirituality."

Religious obsession derailed this family. The husband was using religious scripture to shun his wife's requests for more intimacy in their relationship. He used religion to push her away and to avoid dealing with his own personal issues. On numerous occasions I'd also witnessed him raging at his children. After shouting at them over some small act of immature recklessness, he then sarcastically condemned his wife for not being religious enough. Though he'd memorized volumes of scripture, it was difficult to detect even an ounce of healthy spirituality in this man. Needless to say, his behavior was extremely confusing to our boys. Michael, our children, and I were happy to see him leave our house. Several years later, neither Michael nor I was surprised to learn the couple had divorced.

In the above example, not only did religious obsession destroy a marriage, it set the children up for spiritual problems down the line. Our first concept of a Higher Power or God doesn't come from religion. A child's initial, immature notion of a Higher Power is based on the characteristics of those adults in the child's environment. If a child is abused by an adult, that child may conceive of a Higher Power as a punishing, judgmental God who's to be feared. If our parents are critical, rigid, unavailable, or emotionally abandoning, we'll have a vision of a Higher Power with those features. When our caretakers are supportive, nurturing, and safe, the foundation of our belief in a Higher Power will include supportive, safe, and nurturing characteristics.

Emotionally punishing a child in the name of God can be as devastating as sexual or physical abuse. Children literally believe what their parents tell them. If any caretaker tells a child, "God doesn't like you," the child will believe it. When parents use principles from their religious texts and teachings to shame, threaten, or punish their children, they set religion up as a scary, authoritarian institution.

A parent's rigid religious beliefs can sabotage healthy spiritual development. Religion is an institution that can help us to understand our own spirituality, but when it's abusive or used to control us, it's no longer serving our spiritual development.

Religious Obsession: The Intimacy Stifler

A religiously obsessed person may behave devoutly, but in actuality such behavior is an ineffective shortcut that stunts spiritual growth and delays emotional healing on the inside. For people with abuse or addiction issues who come from religiously obsessed families, or people who have had such partners, the concept of spirituality has to be reexamined for healing to begin. If this doesn't happen, intimacy issues can continue throughout a lifetime.

Religious obsession not only shuts us off from healing difficult life experiences, it creates distance from loved ones. Imperfection is a part of the human condition, and when religion is used to control and manipulate a partner's behavior, intimacy will die and be replaced with dishonesty. It's difficult to experience true intimacy when religious obsession induces a fear of not being good enough. When a couple uses a belief system to hide from relationship issues in need of attention, havoc can result. Unresolved difficulties will be hiding just under the facade of religious perfection. The denial of addiction, past hurt, present anger, or other life problems will also be incredibly strong. With religious self-righteousness, people fool themselves into believing they have been healed when in reality, all they have done is cover up their pain with religion.

A Mask for Unresolved Grief

Comments such as these may indicate unresolved grief masked by religious obsession:

- "Yes, my loved one has died, but she is with God, so why should I feel sad?"

- "I grew up without a mother because she passed when I was just twelve years old, but I don't need to be angry about that. God wouldn't like that."

- "We're losing our house because I lost a well-paying job. The money just isn't coming in like it used to, but I don't have time to be upset. Plus, the universe must have other plans for me, so no tears!"

- "My father recently crossed over after a heart attack, but I'm not grieving. I know he's on the other side in the afterlife, living a wonderful life. I can't be selfish because God must need him more than I do."

- "I'll meet my son in heaven when I die, so I try to not cry over his death."

- "The past is the past. Just stuff away hurt. Help others in the church."

- "My last wife and I will come together again in the next life. We'll be reincarnated together. I refuse to focus in on how I still miss her. Instead I just ignore these feelings and have only joy about our eventual reunion."

- "My husband is an alcoholic, but no, I don't need help. All I can really do is pray. If God loves me my prayers will be answered. God will fix it."

- "I don't have to admit my son is a drug addict. My church group is praying for him and they told me he keeps using drugs because I'm not praying hard enough. I must have made God angry and this is my punishment."

- "This loss is necessary for my growth. To be upset about this shows a lack of faith."

A Mask for Unresolved Anger

When religious obsession shields inner anger, rationalizations like these can result:

- "My loved one is with God. Yes, he was murdered, but why

should I feel mad about never seeing her again? It's God's will."

- "Okay! So she cheated on you! You can't be angry with her for that! It's bad karma! Just move on! Don't bring it up anymore!"

- "My father died when I was very young, and I had to go to work early to take care of my mother. At times I feel angry about my lost youth, but scripture tells me to be grateful for the time I had with him. I ignore my anger, even though my wife says it still comes out sideways."

- "My husband and I aren't as close as we used to be since our daughter's recent passing. I get angry about her death, but my priest tells me to just move on and be a better wife."

- "I know I have a serious illness, but I must be positive at all times! When I feel like crying I tell myself to just stop. The spiritually evolved person weathers these storms with a smile on her face."

- "I'm at peace. Yes, I've been drinking too much, but I'm at peace. My favorite dog died last week but I'm already over it. We'll meet again in the next life. I can't understand why my girl-friend is so upset over this!"

- "Of course I'm angry about losing my job. Wouldn't you be? It wasn't fair and I was mistreated. But my 'angelic guides' are in charge. so I need to just quit whining and get on with life."

- "Positive thinking is a must! No negativity! Feeling anger is giving into the negative. Being angry creates negativity."

- "Anger goes against the teachings of this book I'm reading. The author says, 'There's only love! Think only love! Ignore anger. Only express love towards those who have hurt you!'"

- "Turn the other cheek! Yes, he stole your identity and maxed out your credit cards, but you're a Christian and you need to just forgive him!"

- "If I just pray more and read my Bible, my wife and I will get back together and she'll stop overspending."

- "A therapist told me I was mad at God. She said I was angry because of the sexual abuse I experienced as a child. *I'm not angry!*"

- "I go to church three times a week, but I can't seem to feel connected with any sort of a Higher Power. My dad always said he was God, and he beat me. Now my boyfriend tells me he's king of our castle, but he's a compulsive gambler and I pay the bills! When I remind him of this he uses scripture to tell me he's top dog in this relationship."

A Mask for Hidden Shame

Religion can also be used to hide shame over

- sexual obsession or addiction

- unresolved sexual trauma

- unresolved childhood physical abuse, emotional hurt or trauma

- unaddressed dysfunctional or addictive behavior

Indeed, many abuse survivors use religion to bandage their pain and to avoid confronting the shame, rage, grief, and fear associated with their losses. And we know all too well about the clergy who, behind closed doors, repeat compulsive addictive behaviors themselves. But even for clergy or religiously based counselors who aren't caught in that trap themselves, it is common to misdiagnose relationship problems related to religious obsession.

Recognizing Religious Obsession

Even seasoned relationship therapists have sometimes missed the mark with religiously obsessed individuals or couples. The perfect picture of religious devotion has often fooled members of the mental health community. But finally, individuals and couples suffering from this dysfunction—people who may also be riddled with issues of addiction, trauma, sexual obsession, and unresolved abuse, past or present—are finally beginning to receive psychological attention.

The dysfunction is being forced out of the closet and in recent years, not only have mental health professionals wised up, but religious organizations are becoming more aware of the widespread denial of this issue. Religious communities are recognizing that prayer and attendance at religious services alone won't heal people's personal problems: relationship issues, addictions, painful emotions and losses, childhood abuse, and inappropriate acting out. Many of today's clergy understand that this "blanket obsession" only delays healing and sabotages any chance for true spirituality to blossom. Taking responsibility for our feelings about all of our painful life experiences, past and present, opens us up to healthy intimacy, first with ourselves, then with others and then with our god.

A spiritual person recognizes that intimacy with another requires a sense of connectedness. To feel spiritually linked with the self and others, we must be able to honestly embrace all of our emotions. I believe our ability to experience emotion is a spiritual gift, allowing us to heal from loss, to embrace joy, to learn from life, and to unite with one another. To deprive ourselves of any of our feelings is to distance ourselves from a sense of shared connectedness. In other words, feeling honest emotion can lead to healthy intimacy. Then and only then will we be blessed with true spirituality.

• • •

11

Building Healthy Intimacy

Relationships are part of the vast plan for our enlightenment.

— MARIANNE WILLIAMSON, AUTHOR

Throughout a relationship, seemingly random events can expose our conflicts and remind us that intimacy needs ongoing care and maintenance. One recent example for Michael and me took place in a carpet store.

In September 2008, Hurricane Ike had barreled into Galveston, and, like most of the population, we evacuated. After three weeks we returned home and pumped ten feet of seawater out of our basement. Thanks to flood surges, our oriental carpets were a soggy, moldy mess and we had to replace them. When we decided to purchase new rugs, the long-standing intimacy, love and friendship Michael and I had fostered in our relationship was tested to the limit. Both of us were sad, angry, tired, and overwhelmed. The strain of the storm had finally caught up with us, and in a rug store we found we were at each other's throats! Standing there yelling at each other like a couple of banshees, we realized it was time to get down to business and talk about what was really going on with us.

With healthy intimacy there is a sense of security in the relationship. We can be who we need to be and there are no secrets; we can count on mutual respect, care, and understanding. Once Michael and I sat down on a pile of carpets reminded ourselves of the rules in our "intimacy tool kit," and discussed the post-hurricane stress we were feeling, the fighting stopped. After that, we found several great rugs on sale and had fun doing so. Hurricane Ike almost destroyed our home, but our intimacy tool kit saved our relationship.

An Honest Appraisal

Remember these questions from chapter 1?

- Can I accept or address the problem areas involved in this relationship?

- Will my partner try to work with me in this relationship to move through these difficulties?

- Are both of us committed to growing together?

Do you remember how you initially answered these questions? As you look at them now, do you think would your answers be the same? So many of us know almost nothing about what true, honest, intimate communication with others—or even with the self—is all about. All relationships have problems, but many of us don't understand that there are answers to most relationship issues. Too many couples call it quits and begin the chase again. As we have seen, this is never the solution.

In my clinical practice with those who do stay together, the partner who is in more pain about the relationship is often the first to seek treatment. Rarely do I see both partners walking hand in hand through the door of my office, prepared to work together. Recognize that if your partner isn't ready to join you in addressing the intimacy issues in your relationship, you can begin yourself. Learning how to first take care of ourselves often lays the necessary groundwork for our partners to eventually recognize they too need healing.

When both individuals are working together toward improving intimacy in the relationship, it's time to start putting together your own unique Intimacy Tool Kit. Over a period of time Michael and I put together our own kit. When Hurricane Ike flooded our home, Michael and I dug deep into that kit to maintain open communication, a sense of compassion for one another, and the ability to effectively resolve disagreements and respectfully work together as best friends. Each of us needed to be individually responsible for our own addictions without misdirecting painful emotions onto one another. One more time, our Tool Kit worked great. Now I'd like to share with you the initial steps we took to begin developing these intimacy skills, starting with a few rules.

The Intimacy Tool Kit:
Beginning Rules for a Healthy Relationship

Remember these five general rules as you build intimacy: they will serve you well. *Friendship comes first. Communicate. Be respectful. Practice self-care. And don't give up!*

Friendship comes first.

- Learn how to be friends before becoming lovers.

- Have a date night at least once a week, and take turns planning the activities and meals.

- If you argue during a date night, it's okay.

- Try new hobbies together.

- Take quiet time to connect with each other every day.

- Understand that best friends disagree from time to time.

Communicate.

- Be an active listener.

- Be open and direct.

- Try to stick to the facts, and state only your own feelings.

- Don't interrupt your partner when speaking.

- Don't put issues on a back burner, thinking they will go away.

- Stay in the here and now.

- If you're unsure you understand, repeat back what you heard.

- Discuss only one topic at a time.

- Resolve one issue at a time.

Be respectful.

- Avoid being judgmental.
- Watch for hidden resentment.
- Don't shame your partner.
- Respectfully share your concerns and ideas.
- Be aware of feelings.
- No unfair, below-the-belt comments.
- Don't use sex or money as a weapon.
- Be assertive when you need to be, but not overly pushy or aggressive.
- Try to not overreact, and don't retaliate by attacking.
- Avoid out-shouting your partner.

Practice self-care.

- Take space from one another if you need to.
- Sleep in separate rooms when you're at an impasse.
- Don't have sex with your partner if you don't want to.
- Never use sex to fix a disagreement.
- Avoid panicking if there is a rise in conversational noise level.
- If shouting is being used to shut you out, take space.
- If hurtful raging begins, take personal space.
- Don't accept emotional or physical abuse.

Don't give up.

- Recognize that it's okay to have differing opinions.
- Be clear on what your disagreements are really about.
- Write your feelings out in letters if you feel misunderstood.
- Understand that there doesn't have to be a winner.

- Compromise with one another.

- Connect with a supportive friend if you need to.

- Get professional help when you feel stuck.

- Continue to take responsibility for your own healing.

Taking Responsibility for Healing

If we have addiction issues, what are we willing to do about them? By taking responsibility for our behavior, we're not only improving our chances for an intimate relationship, but we're also taking care of ourselves. When we take care of ourselves we develop a sense of self-love and begin to fill the emptiness our past and present hurts have created. By being responsible for our actions, we no longer have to be in pain or hurt those we love, because we've learned how to respect others and love ourselves. Many of us have spent years living in shame, with feelings of unworthiness and loneliness. We've tried to use relationships to make us feel complete, but in the end the pain has only grown.

That's why we often need the help of others to assist us along the path of healing. Working with a professional or with the aid of a support group gives us a chance to address our shame, pain, anger, and sense of isolation in a safe and supportive environment. Sharing our feelings with those who understand helps us see we're not alone and that healing is possible. When we begin to heal as individuals, movement toward healthy intimacy with others will also begin.

The next step depends on whether you and your partner are willing to work together. Remember: a healthy relationship involves two emotionally whole people coming together to share a journey as they continue to grow as individuals. But often we seem to believe that a relationship is healthy when two incomplete people come together to try to complete one another. We give up the parts of ourselves that are necessary for our individual development. If that's been happening, we need to take steps to heal. If our partner isn't willing, we can start the process on our own. Often, partners will get into their own healing when we stop enabling them and start taking care of ourselves.

Now, based on what you've read in this book and what you've learned from reviewing the above intimacy concerns, find out what your next step will be by taking a pen and paper and answering these final questions.

1. List what you believe your addictions and issues might be.

2. List what you believe your present partner's addictions and issues are (or answer for a past partner, if you're examining a past relationship).

3. List what you need to do to be responsible for your own addictions and issues.

4. List what you need (or needed) to do to quit enabling your partner's addictions and issues.

If your relationship has ended, you might be feeling that you don't really know who you are, where your life is going, or what it is you want. As far as you are concerned, the end of your relationship translates into the end of who you are. Why do we think this way? Feeling very sad at the end of a relationship is normal, but many of us have lost ourselves to the relationship and allowed our partner to define us, so the end feels like death. We feel emotionally, physically, and spiritually incapacitated and don't know how we can go on. Some of us take to the bed, stop eating, eat too much, isolate from friends, drink too much, or seek out strong pharmaceuticals. We feel this way because when we lost the relationship, our identity went with it. When this happens, extreme steps must often be taken, even when we don't feel like doing so.

Though the following steps can apply to any difficult relationship, if you have just suffered a relationship breakup and don't know what to do next, I strongly encourage you to review these questions—and note the suggested answers.

What steps do you commit to taking to begin healing yourself?

1. Go to a Twelve Step or other support group? *Yes!*

2. Find a therapist who understands obsessive behaviors and addictive relationships? *Yes!*

3. Look into workshops or treatment for obsessive, addictive, and co-addict behavior? *Yes!*

4. Educate yourself on obsessive behavior patterns, addictions, and co-addictive reactions? *Yes!*

5. Wait for your partner to "get it" or for the perfect partner to materialize? *No!*

Commitment to repairing a damaged relationship as a couple takes courage, perseverance, and dedication. Grief and resentments take time to resolve, and trust isn't built overnight. Patience is the key to successful healing for a couple. As both partners start to share feelings about the relationship, angry emotions are bound to surface. Because of this, commitment is needed. When airing old relationship hurts, threats such as "I'll leave!" or "Let's get a divorce!" can sabotage any healthy resolution. To avoid that, I suggest you agree that no mention of abandoning the relationship will be made for six months. After that, you can reevaluate and discuss whether to continue the relationship or end it. Even if the decision is to end the relationship, at least both partners will have had time to explore any childhood history that set up their intimacy difficulties. If one member refuses to explore, then the other person will hopefully have done some work and have an understanding of why the relationship didn't work. In the future, this person will be better prepared for the next relationship.

Your Healing Journey Continues

Each time we start a new relationship, we take ourselves with us. And so it's our job to learn how to be whole human beings who are capable of parenting ourselves within our relationships. When we learn how to love ourselves, to take care of our own needs, and to take responsibility for those actions of ours that hurt, enable, or upset others, we discover we don't need our partner to make us feel okay about who we are. This frees us from being disappointed when our partner can't fulfill all of our wants, expectations, and desires.

Love doesn't begin with the perfect partner. That initial sense of perfection is just the chemical illusion of lust, and those hormones eventually wear off. Healthy love begins when we learn how to appreciate and accept who we are, with all our talents and imperfections. As we discover how to cherish and love ourselves, we'll learn how to nurture and care for others. With a love of the self, we'll finally be ready for the wonderful experience of connectedness and intimacy with another human being.

This book is just the beginning. You've been given the tools to start the good work. Pick them up, bravely examine your history and how your relationships may have replayed your painful past. If you do this, your chances will be better than excellent for a successful, healthy, intimate, truly loving experience in the near future. Embrace your destiny and continue your healing! Don't stop here!

• • •

Barriers to Intimacy Worksheets

How will you heal your intimacy issues and improve your chances for a healthy relationship? You can only do this by looking at you, so where will you begin? Answer the questions on the worksheets that follow as honestly as you can. It's best to write out your answers on paper, but some of my clients have found it useful to simply read them and answer them mentally.

When thinking about your responses, watch out for the following tricks that we sometimes play on ourselves:

- **Minimization:** underestimating or downplaying an issue. For example: "My mother's alcoholism didn't really affect me that much."

- **Rationalization:** giving reasons that may be plausible, but are really untrue or beside the point. For example: "My wife had an affair, but that's over and done with. We don't need to talk about it."

- **Justification:** vindicating or making excuses in an underhanded way. For example: "My dad was never at home and always at work, so I never saw him. But this didn't hurt me. He had to pay the bills."

- **Denial:** refusing to admit the truth or reality of a situation. For example: "My partner has a best friend who is always visiting her. Even though she spends more time with him than with me, I know nothing is going on."

WORKSHEET FOR CHAPTER 2:

How We Learn about Relationships

Begin your healing by digging deeper into how you learned about intimate relationships. Let's start with a few simple exploratory questions about your family of origin history.

- Are your parents married to one another, and if so, for how many years?

- If they divorced, do you know why they separated?

- Did one parent die before the other?

- If either has remarried, how healthy are these marriages?

- If you don't have an active relationship with your parents, why not?

- If you were not raised by your parents, who brought you up?

- What were these relationships like? Are you still in contact with these caregivers?

We learn about feeling and expressing emotion by watching our parents. If we were not raised by our biological parents, we learn about feelings by observing those who raised us. Even if our caregivers or adoptive parents were wonderful people, if they had problems, those issues can impact us. When answering the following questions, answer for your biological parents or for those who raised you.

Let's start with your dad, stepdad, granddad, or other male caregivers. Gay families may have a dad and a "dad two."

- How did your dad act when he was happy, sad, frustrated, upset, angry, grieving a death or loss, ill, feeling out of control, or irritated with the other parent? Do you still see these patterns today?

- Could your father talk about anything with you, or did he avoid some issues? Is that still true today?

- Could you talk to him about these topics? Is that still true today?
    - any areas of disagreement
    - your own disappointments or problems
    - health issues
    - addictions (alcohol, drugs, food, sex, work, and so on)
    - sex
    - religion
    - politics
    - past family history
    - his childhood
    - abuses or tragedies he has experienced
    - his relationships with parents and relatives
- Growing up, what did you like about your father, and what did you dislike? Is that still true today?
- How often did you talk to him growing up? Today?
- Could your father possibly have had addictions in any of these areas, either now or in the past? If so, what have been the effects been on you? (Check those that apply.)
    - ☐ alcohol
    - ☐ drugs, either illegal or prescription
    - ☐ sex
    - ☐ relationships or affairs
    - ☐ one-night stands or prostitutes
    - ☐ pornography
    - ☐ gambling
    - ☐ work
    - ☐ housecleaning or busy work
    - ☐ hobbies
    - ☐ overinvolvement in causes or activities

☐ martyrdom or self-pity

☐ depressive behavior

☐ angry behavior

☐ exercise

☐ eating too little or too much

☐ bulimic behavior

☐ religious activities

☐ shopping or compulsive spending

☐ other (name them yourself)

Now let's look at some additional factors that can affect relationships. (Check those that apply to your father.)

☐ immigrant status, especially for the first generation from another country

☐ syndrome

☐ death of spouse or a child

☐ surviving the Great Depression

☐ financial difficulties

☐ controlling behavior

☐ illegal activity or prison time

☐ work-related problems

☐ tendency to take care of others but neglect family

☐ trouble sitting still

☐ weight problems

☐ chronic illness

☐ chronic depression; bipolar disorder

☐ hospitalizations for mental illness

Let's now look briefly at your father's parents.

• Are your paternal grandparents still alive? Does (or did) your father have a good relationship with them?

• If not, do you know why not? How has this affected him?

• What difficulties are you aware of with regard to your paternal grandparents? Let's start with the same possible addiction issues noted above with regard to your father. (Check those that apply and list which grandparent had each problem.)

☐ alcohol _____

☐ drugs, either illegal or prescription _____

☐ sex _____

☐ relationships or affairs _____

☐ one-night stands or prostitutes _____

☐ pornography _____

☐ gambling _____

☐ work _____

☐ housecleaning or busy work _____

☐ hobbies _____

☐ overinvolvement in causes or activities _____

☐ martyrdom or self-pity _____

☐ depressive behavior _____

☐ angry behavior _____

☐ exercise _____

☐ eating too little or too much _____

☐ bulimic behavior _____

☐ religious activities _____

☐ shopping or compulsive spending _____

☐ other (name them yourself) _____

And now let's look at some additional factors that can affect relationships. (Check those that apply and list which grandparent.)

☐ immigrant status, especially
   for the first generation
   from another country   _____

☐ war veteran status; possible
   post-traumatic stress syndrome   _____

☐ death of spouse or a child   _____

☐ surviving the Great Depression   _____

☐ financial difficulties   _____

☐ controlling behavior   _____

☐ illegal activity or prison time   _____

☐ work-related problems   _____

☐ tendency to take care of others
   but neglect family   _____

☐ trouble sitting still   _____

☐ weight problems   _____
☐ chronic illness   _____

☐ chronic depression; bipolar
   disorder   _____

☐ hospitalizations for mental
   illness   _____

- How did the above impact your father?

- How did your father's relationship with his father affect him? Has this affected you, and if so, how?

- How did your father's relationship with his mother affect him? Has this affected you, and if so, how?

Let's continue with your mom, stepmom, grandmother, or other female caregivers. Gay families may have a mom and a "mom two."

- How did your mom act when she was happy, sad, frustrated, upset, angry, grieving a death or loss, ill, feeling out of control, or irritated with the other parent? Do you still see these patterns today?

- Could your mother talk about anything with you, or did she avoid some issues? Is that still true today?

- Could you talk to her about these topics? Is that still true today?
  - any areas of disagreement
  - your own disappointments or problems
  - health issues
  - addictions (alcohol, drugs, food, sex, work, and so on)
  - sex
  - religion
  - politics
  - past family history
  - her childhood
  - abuses or tragedies she has experienced
  - her relationships with parents and relatives

- Growing up, what did you like about your mother, and what did you dislike? Is that still true today?

- How often did you talk to her growing up? Today?

- Could your mother possibly have had addictions in any of these areas, either now or in the past? If so, what have been the effects been on you? (Check those that apply.)
  - ☐ alcohol
  - ☐ drugs, either illegal or prescription
  - ☐ sex
  - ☐ relationships or affairs
  - ☐ one-night stands or prostitutes
  - ☐ pornography

☐ gambling

☐ work

☐ housecleaning or busy work

☐ hobbies

☐ overinvolvement in causes or activities

☐ martyrdom or self-pity

☐ depressive behavior

☐ angry behavior

☐ exercise

☐ eating too little or too much

☐ bulimic behavior

☐ religious activities

☐ shopping or compulsive spending

☐ other (name them yourself) _____

Now let's look at some additional factors that can affect relationships:

☐ immigrant status, especially for the first generation from another country

☐ war veteran status; possible post-traumatic stress syndrome

☐ death of spouse or a child

☐ surviving the Great Depression

☐ financial difficulties

☐ controlling behavior

☐ illegal activity or prison time

☐ work-related problems

☐ tendency to take care of others but neglect family

☐ trouble sitting still

☐ weight problems

☐ chronic illness

☐ chronic depression; bipolar disorder

☐ hospitalizations for mental illness

Now look briefly at your mother's parents.

- Are your maternal grandparents still alive? Does (or did) your mother have a good relationship with them?

- If not, do you know why not? How has this affected her?

- What difficulties are you aware of with regard to your maternal grandparents? Let's start with the same possible addiction issues noted above with regard to your mother. (Check those that apply and list which grandparent had each problem.)

☐ alcohol   _____

☐ drugs, either illegal or prescription   _____

☐ sex   _____

☐ relationships or affairs   _____

☐ one-night stands or prostitutes   _____

☐ pornography   _____

☐ gambling   _____

☐ work   _____

☐ housecleaning or busy work   _____

☐ hobbies   _____

☐ overinvolvement in causes or activities   _____

☐ martyrdom or self-pity   _____

☐ depressive behavior   _____

☐ angry behavior   _____

☐ exercise   _____

☐ eating too little or too much   _____

☐ bulimic behavior   _____

☐ religious activities   _____

☐ shopping or compulsive spending   _____

☐ other (name them yourself)   _____

Now let's look at some additional factors that can affect relationships:

☐ immigrant status, especially for the first generation from another country

☐ war veteran status; possible post-traumatic stress syndrome

☐ death of spouse or a child

☐ surviving the Great Depression

☐ financial difficulties

☐ controlling behavior

☐ illegal activity or prison time

☐ work-related problems

☐ tendency to take care of others but neglect family

☐ trouble sitting still

☐ weight problems

☐ chronic illness

☐ chronic depression; bipolar disorder

☐ hospitalizations for mental illness

Communication between Mom and Dad

• Do you know how your parents discussed with one another the following topics while you were growing up? Today?

☐ money problems

☐ children

☐ relatives and family problems

☐ household chores

☐ education

☐ sex

☐ illness

☐ employment

☐ religion

☐ fears or worries

☐ legal issues

☐ death

- When your parents fought, who usually won and why? Still true today?

- Did your parents resolve their disagreements, or did they fight the same fights over and over again? Still true today?

- Was there violence, either emotional or physical? How did you feel about this?

- If they didn't fight, how could you tell when they were angry with each other?

- Which parent did you feel safer with and why? Still true today?

- Did your parents kiss, hug, or flirt with each other in front of you? Still true today?

- Are you aware of any family secrets, and if so how do you feel about these?

- Close your eyes and imagine your parents having sex. What happens when you do this? You've just peeked at your view of them as sexual beings. Do you see warmth, or rigidity? What did you see?

For more information on specific addictions and family-of-origin difficulties, read *Natural Mental Health: How to Take Control of Your Own Emotional Well-Being* by Carla Wills-Brandon.

• • •

Alcohol and Other Drug Addiction

In reading this book, you may have discovered that you have some issues of chemical dependency with your current or past partners. Review this list and see what you discover. Circle Yes or No for each question.

Is Your Partner Chemically Dependent?

1. Have you ever been uneasy with your partner's alcohol or drug consumption? Yes No

2. Has anyone ever expressed concern about your partner's alcohol or drug consumption? Yes No

3. Do you feel embarrassed when you are in public and your partner is intoxicated or behaving poorly because of drug or alcohol use? Yes No

4. Are you uneasy or even fearful when driving with your partner after drugs or alcohol has been ingested? Yes No

5. Have you ever tried to "keep up" or connect with your partner by drinking or using drugs when you didn't want to? Yes No

6. Are you worried about the number of mood-altering prescription medications your partner is taking? Yes No

7. Has drug or alcohol use ever interfered with your sex life? Yes No

8. Do you feel your partner does not hear you, understand you, spend enough quality time with you or help you enough with day to day tasks? Yes No

9. Are you lonely in your relationship, even when your partner is physically present? Yes No

10. Have your parents, friends or other family members expressed concern for your well-being in this relationship? Yes No

11. When your partner is late arriving home, or if you can't get in touch with him or her, do you find yourself thinking the worst has happened? Yes No

12. Has your partner ever told you that you are mistaken about certain events or conversations, indicating they never happened because he or she doesn't remember them? Yes No Do you then question your own memory? Yes No

13. Do you find yourself taking on more responsibility around the house, with finances, or with children because your partner has slacked off? Yes No

14. Have you made excuses to family, friends, coworkers, your children or your partner's employer for behavior which is related to drinking or drug use? Yes No

15. Do you believe if you just tried harder and could make your spouse understand how you feel, he or she would finally see just how unhappy you are? Do you find yourself making certain careful statements, couching your words, avoiding particular topics, or watching your voice intonation or mannerisms in ways that seem overly self-conscious? Yes No

Did you answer yes to three or more of the above? If you did, your partner just might be chemically dependent, and you may want to suggest he or she get a professional assessment. If your partner resists, of if the assessment confirms chemical dependency and your partner still refuses to get help, you should find support yourself through counseling and attending a support group such as Al-Anon.

· · ·

Work Addiction

Are you or your partner work addicted or overdoing it? Take the Work Addiction Risk Test—also known as the WART Inventory—and see!

Work Addiction Risk Test (WART Inventory)[*]

Read each of the following 25 statements and decide how much each one pertains to you. Use the following scale to answer each question and keep track of your score.

The statement is true of me:

    1 = Never

    2 = Sometimes

    3 = Often true

    4 = Always true

1. ___ I prefer to do most things myself rather than ask for help.

2. ___ I get very impatient when I have to wait for someone else or when something takes too long, such as long, slow-moving lines.

3. ___ I seem to be in a hurry, racing against the clock.

4. ___ I get irritated when I am interrupted while I am in the middle of something.

5. ___ I stay busy and keep many "irons in the fire."

6. ___ I find myself doing two or three things at one time, such as eating lunch and writing a memo while talking on the phone.

7. ___ I overcommit myself by biting off more than I can chew.

8. ___ I feel guilty when I am not working on something.

9. ___ It's important that I see the concrete results of what I do.

10. ___ I am more interested in the final results of my work than in the process.

11. ___ Things just never seem to move fast enough or get done fast enough for me.

12. ___ I lose my temper when things don't go my way or work out to suit me.

13. ___ I ask the same question, without realizing it, after I've already been given the answer.

14. ___ I spend a lot of time mentally planning and thinking about future events, while tuning out the here and now.

15. ___ I find myself continuing to work after my coworkers have called it quits.

16. ___ I get angry when people don't meet my standards of perfection.

17. ___ I get upset when I am in situations where I cannot be in control.

18. ___ I tend to put myself under pressure with self-imposed deadlines.

19. ___ It is hard for me to relax when I'm not working.

20. ___ I spend more time working than socializing with friends or pursuing hobbies and leisure activities.

21. ___ I dive into projects to get a head start before all the phases have been finalized.

22. ___ I get upset with myself for making even the smallest mistake.

23. ___ I put more thought, time, and energy into my work than I do into my relationships with friends and loved ones.

24. ___ I forget, ignore, or minimize important family celebrations such as birthdays, reunions, anniversaries, or holidays.

25. ___ I make important decisions before I have all the facts and have a chance to think them through thoroughly.

Now, add up the numbers in the blanks for your score.
Total Score: ___

Score 25 – 49: You are not overdoing it.
Congratulations! You've achieved a balance between getting things done and taking time for yourself. Keep it up!

Score 50 – 69: You are mildly overdoing it.
You're doing really well, but be careful. You have a tendency to become very busy. Take time for the things that are important to you, and don't be afraid to say no.

Score 70 – 100: You are highly overdoing it.
Well, you're too busy, but you probably knew that already. Read the chapter titled "Risky Busyness" in *Chained to the Desk* for suggestions on how you can tailor your activities to meet your life goals.

• • •

Sexual Obsession and Cybersex Addiction

Do you know the signs and symptoms of cybersex addiction? The following is an excellent guide for examining this potential intimacy blocker.

Cybersex Addiction Screening Test [*]
By Robert Weiss, LCSW, CAS

The Cybersex Addiction Screening Test is designed to assist the assessment of sexually compulsive or "addictive" behavior. The test provides a profile of responses that help to identify men and women with sexually addictive disorders. Check each "Yes" response as appropriate. [For confidential results, answer the following questions online at http://www.sexualrecovery.com/resources/selftests/csat.php.]

1. Do you spend increasing amounts of online time focused on sexual or romantic intrigue or involvement? ☐ Yes

2. Are you involved in multiple romantic or sexual affairs in chat rooms, Internet or BBS [bulletin board system]? ☐ Yes

3. Do you not consider online sexual or romantic "affairs" to be a possible violation of spousal/partnership commitments? ☐ Yes

4. Have you failed in attempts to cut back on frequency of online or Internet sexual and romantic involvement or interaction? ☐ Yes

5. Does online use interfere with work (tired or late due to previous night's use, online while at work, etc.)? ☐ Yes

6. Does online use interfere with primary relationships (e.g., minimizing or lying to partners about online activities, spending less time with family or partners)? ☐ Yes

7. Are you intensely engaged in collecting Internet pornography? ☐ Yes

8. Do you engage in fantasy online acts or experiences that would be illegal if carried out (e.g., rape, child molestation)? □ Yes

9. Has your social or family interactive time decreased due to online fantasy involvement? □ Yes

10. Are you secretive, or do you lie about the amount of time spent online or type of sexual/romantic fantasy activities carried out online? □ Yes

11. Do you engage with sexual or romantic partners met online, while also involved in marital or other primary relationship? □ Yes

12. Are there increasing numbers of complaints or concerns from family or friends about the amount of time spent online? □ Yes

13. Do you frequently become angry or extremely irritable when asked to give up online involvement to engage with partners, family or friends? □ Yes

14. Has the primary focus of sexual or romantic life become increasingly related to computer activity (including pornographic CD-ROM use)? □ Yes

---

*The Cybersex Addiction Screening Test was developed by Robert Weiss, LCSW, CAS, director of the Sexual Recovery Institute. It is used here with author permission. Robert Weiss can be reached at www.sexualrecovery.com.

For further information on cybersex and sexual addiction, read Patrick Carnes's *Out of the Shadows: Understanding Sexual Addiction,* 3rd ed. (Center City, MN: Hazelden, 2001).

Self-Help Resources

This book was just a beginning, and now it's time for you to spread your wings and fly. Remember, you deserve an intimate relationship, but only you can make this happen.

Over the last twenty-five years I've created a resource list that I use regularly with those who visit my office, and now I'd like to share it with you. I suggest you take a few moments to look at each of the resources below. Go to the Web sites and explore the information offered by each organization. Check out the suggested readings. While going through the list, trust your gut. If it feels right, it's probably right for you. Though some of the suggestions might seem unfamiliar, others will feel perfectly tailored to meet your needs.

Author's Contact Information

Carla Wills-Brandon

281-338-2992

beyondthechase@sbcglobal.net.

Chemical Addiction

Alcoholics Anonymous

P.O. Box 459

New York, NY 10163

212-870-3400

www.aa.org

Cocaine Anonymous
3740 Overland Avenue, Suite C
Los Angeles, CA 90034-6337
310-559-5833
http://ca.org

Crystal Meth Anonymous
4470 West Sunset Boulevard, Suite 107
PMB 555
Los Angeles, CA 90027-6302
213-488-4455 (hotline)
www.crystalmeth.org

Marijuana Anonymous World Services
P.O. Box 2912
Van Nuys, CA 91404
800-766-6779
www.marijuana-anonymous.org

Narcotics Anonymous
P.O. Box 9999
Van Nuys, CA 91409
818-773-9999
www.na.org

National Alcohol and Drug Abuse Foundation
1-800-784-6776

**National Council on Alcoholism
and Drug Dependence (NCADD)**
244 East 58th Street, 4th Floor
New York, NY 10022
212-269-7797
www.ncadd.org

Pills Anonymous

www.pillsanonymous.info

Suggested Readings

Kurtz, Ernest, and Katherine Ketcham. *The Spirituality of Imperfection: Storytelling and the Search for Meaning.* New York: Bantam, 1993.

Z., Michael. *The Wisdom of the Rooms: A Year of Weekly Reflections.* Palm Tree Press, 2007.

Families and Mental/Emotional Health

Attention Deficit Disorder Association (ADDA)

P.O. Box 7557
Wilmington, DE 19803
800-939-1019
www.add.org

Autism Society of America (ASA)

7910 Woodmont Avenue, Suite 300
Bethesda, MD 20814
800-328-8476
www.autism-society.org

**Children and Adults with Attention Deficit/
Hyperactivity Disorder (CHADD)**

8181 Professional Place, Suite 150
Landover, MD 20785
301-306-7070
http://chadd.org

Families Anonymous

P.O. Box 3475
Culver City, CA 90231-3475
800-736-9805
www.familiesanonymous.org

Parent Soup Message Boards

This URL redirects the user to online message boards dealing with parenting and family issues.

www.parentsoup.com/boards

Parental Stress Service

22455 Maple Court, Suite 402

Hayward, CA 94541

510-582-0148

800-829-3777 (crisis line)

www.psshelps.org/familyhot.htm

Parents Anonymous

675 West Foothill Boulevard, Suite 220

Claremont, CA 91711

909-621-6184

www.parentsanonymous.org

Parents without Partners

1650 South Dixie Highway, Suite 402

Boca Raton, FL 33432

800-637-7974

www.parentswithoutpartners.org

Suggested Reading

Bradshaw, John. *Family Secrets: The Path from Shame to Healing.* New York: Bantam, 1996.

Burns, Diane Drake. *Autism? Asperger's? ADHD? ADD?* Arlington, TX: Future Horizons, 2005.

Wallerstein, Judith S., Julia M. Lewis, and Sandra Blakeslee. *The Unexpected Legacy of Divorce: The 25-Year Landmark Study* New York: Hyperion, 2001.

Eating Disorders

Anorexics and Bulimics Anonymous
780-443-6077
www.anorexicsandbulimicsanonymousaba.com

Eating Disorders Anonymous (EDA)
www.eatingdisordersanonymous.org

Food Addicts in Recovery Anonymous
400 West Cummings Park, Suite 1700
Woburn, MA 01801
781-932-6300
www.foodaddicts.org

National Eating Disorders Association (NEDA)
603 Stewart Street, Suite 803
Seattle, WA 98101
800-931-2237
www.nationaleatingdisorders.org

Overeaters Anonymous
P.O. Box 44020
Rio Rancho, NM 87174-4020
505-891-2664
www.oa.org

Suggested Readings
Danowski, Debbie, and Pedro Lazaro. *Why Can't I Stop Eating? Recognizing, Understanding, and Overcoming Food Addiction.* Center City, MN: Hazelden, 2000.

L., Elizabeth. *Food for Thought: Daily Meditations for Overeaters.* Center City, MN: Hazelden, 1980.

Family and Friends of Addicted Persons

Adult Children of Alcoholics
P.O. Box 3216
Torrance, CA 90510
310-534-1815
www.adultchildren.org

Al-Anon Family Group Headquarters
1600 Corporate Landing Parkway
Virginia Beach, VA 23454-5617
757-563-1600
www.al-anon.org

Co-Anon Family Groups (Family and Friends of Cocaine Addicts)
P.O. Box 12722
Tucson, AZ 85732-2722
800-898-9985
www.co-anon.org

Families Anonymous (for those close to people with drug, alcohol, or behavior problems)
P.O. Box 3475Culver City, CA 90231-3475
800-736-9805
www.FamiliesAnonymous.org

Nar-Anon Family Groups
22527 Crenshaw Boulevard, Suite 200B
Torrance, CA 90505
800-477-6291
www.nar-anon.org

Suggested Reading
Conyers, Beverly. *Addict in the Family: Stories of Loss, Hope, and Recovery.* Center City, MN: Hazelden, 2003.

Miller, Angelyn. *The Enabler: When Helping Hurts the Ones You Love.* Wheatmark, 2001.

Family Violence

Batterers Anonymous
1040 South Mt. Vernon Avenue, G-306
Colton, CA 92324
951-312-1041

Domestic Abuse Helpline for Men and Women (DAHMW)
Box 252
Harmony, ME 04942
888-743-5754
http://dahmw.org

Pathways to Peace, Inc. (self-help anger management and violence prevention programs)
P.O. Box 259
Cassadaga, NY 14718
800-775-4212
www.pathwaystopeaceinc.com

The Healing Club (domestic violence online support group)
820 South Monaco Parkway, Suite 272
Denver, CO 80224
800-590-3233
www.healingclub.com

Support Network for Battered Women
1257 Tasman Drive, Suite C
Sunnyvale, CA 94089
800-572-2782 (24-hour helpline)
www.snbw.org

Suggested Reading

Engel, Beverly. *The Emotionally Abusive Relationship: How to Stop Being Abused and How to Stop Abusing.* Hoboken, NJ: Wiley, 2003.

Fourre, Constance. *Finding Your Way through Domestic Abuse: A Guide to Physical, Emotional, and Spiritual Healing.* Notre Dame, IN: Ave Maria Press, 2006.

Mental Health Resources

American Mental Health Foundation
212-737-9027
http://americanmentalhealthfoundation.org

Anxiety Disorders Association of America (ADAA)
8730 Georgia Avenue, Suite 600
Silver Spring, MD 20910
240-485-1001
www.adaa.org

Depressed Anonymous
P.O. Box 17414
Louisville, KY 40217
502-569-1989
www.depressedanon.com

Dep-Anon (Family and Friends of Depressed Persons)
P.O. Box 17414
Louisville, KY 40217
www.depressedanon.com

Emotional Health Anonymous
P.O. Box 2081
San Gabriel, CA 91778
626-287-6260
http://home.flash.net/~sgveha/index.htm

Emotions Anonymous
P.O. Box 4245
St. Paul, MN 55104-0245
651-647-9712
www.emotionsanonymous.org

National Institute of Mental Health (NIMH)
6001 Executive Boulevard
Bethesda, MD 20892-9663
www.nimh.nih.gov

Obsessive-Compulsive Anonymous
P.O. Box 215
New Hyde Park, NY 11040
516-739-0662
www.obsessivecompulsiveanonymous.org

Suggested Readings
Bourne, Edmund J., Arlen Brownstein, and Lorna Garano. *Natural Relief for Anxiety: Complementary Strategies for Easing Fear, Panic & Worry.* Oakland, CA: New Harbinger, 2004.

O., Jack. *Dealing with Depression, in Twelve Step Recovery Fellow Travelers Series.* Center City, MN: Hazelden, 2001.

Miscellaneous Self-Help

Adrenaline Addicts Anonymous
350 South Center Street, Suite 500
Reno, NV 89501
www.adrenalineaddicts.org

Debtors Anonymous (credit card debt and money issues)
General Service Office
P.O. Box 920888

Needham, MA 02492-0009

800-421-2383

www.debtorsanonymous.org

Gamblers Anonymous

P.O. Box 17173

Los Angeles, CA 90017

213-386-8789

www.gamblersanonymous.org

Gam-Anon Family Groups (friends and family of addicted gamblers)

P.O Box 157

Whitestone, NY 11357

718-352-1671

www.gam-anon.org

Workaholics Anonymous

P.O. Box 289

Menlo Park, CA 94026-0289

510-273-9253

www.workaholics-anonymous.org

Suggested Readings

Hirschfield, Jerry. *The Twelve Steps for Everyone . . . who really wants them.* Rev. ed. Center City, MN: Hazelden, 1976.

Relationship Support

Co-Dependents Anonymous (CoDA)

P.O. Box 33577

Phoenix, AZ 85067-3577

602-277-7991

www.coda.org

Divorce Anonymous
18 West Street
Annapolis, MD 21401
www.divorceanonymous.com

Love Addicts Anonymous
www.loveaddicts.org

Sex and Love Addicts Anonymous
www.slaafws.org

Recovering Couples Anonymous
P.O. Box 11029
Oakland, CA 94611
510-663-2312
www.recovering-couples.org

HCV: Hepatitis C Anonymous
129 West Canada
San Clemente, CA 92672
949-264-4175
www.hcvanonymous.com

HIV/AIDS: HIV Anonymous
129 West Canada
San Clemente,CA 92672
949-264-4170
www.hivanonymous.com

HerpeSite.org (herpes online personal empowerment and support)
www.herpesite.org

American Social Health Association (ASHA) Hotline
P.O. Box 13827
Research Triangle Park, NC 27709
1-800-227-8922
http://www.ashastd.org/

Suggested Readings

Carnes, Stephanie, Ed. *Mending a Shattered Heart: A Guide for Partners of Sex Addicts.* Gentle Path Press, 2008.

Dawson, Emma. *My Secret Life with a Sex Addict.* Thornton Publishing, 2004.

Jenkins, Mark. *Hepatitis C: Practical, Medical, and Spiritual Guidelines for Daily Living with HCV,* Hazelden Pocket Health Guide. Center City, MN: Hazelden, 2000.

Jenkins, Mark. *HIV/AIDS: Practical, Medical, and Spiritual Guidelines for Daily Living When You're HIV-Positive,* Hazelden Pocket Health Guide. Center City, MN: Hazelden, 2000.

Sexual Abuse and Incest

Incest Survivors Anonymous
P.O. Box 17245
Long Beach, CA 90807-7245
562-428-5599
www.lafn.org/medical/isa

Survivors of Incest Anonymous
P.O. Box 190
Benson, MD 21018-9998
410-893-3322
www.siawso.org

Suggested Readings

Adams, Jada. *The Colors Within: One Rainbow Reclaimed.* Xlibris, 2006.

Bass, Ellen, and Laura Davis. *The Courage to Heal: A Guide for Women Survivors of Child Sexual Abuse.* 20th Anniversary Ed. New York: HarperCollins, 2008.

Sexual Healing

COSA (formerly Co-dependents of Sexual Addicts)
International Service Organization of COSA
P.O. Box 14537
Minneapolis, MN 55414
763-537-6904
www.cosa-recovery.org/home.html

Porn Addicts Anonymous
http://pornaddictsanonymous.org

Sex Addicts Anonymous
ISO of SAA
P.O. Box 70949
Houston, TX 77270
800-477-8191 (U.S. and Canada)
713-869-4902
www.saa-recovery.org

SexHelp.Com
http://sexhelp.com/addiction_definitions.cfm

Sexual Compulsives Anonymous
P.O. Box 1585, Old Chelsea Station
New York, NY 10011
800-977-4325 (800-977-HEAL)
www.sca-recovery.org

Sexual Recovery Institute
822 S. Robertson Boulevard, Suite 303
Los Angeles, CA 90035
310-360-0130
www.sexualrecovery.com

Society for the Advancement of Sexual Health (SASH)
P.O. Box 433
Royston, GA 30662
706-356-7031
www.sash.net

Suggested Reading

Leahy, Michael, *Porn Nation: Conquering America's #1 Addiction.* Chicago: Northfield, 2008.

Weiss, Robert, and Jennifer P. Schneider, *Untangling the Web: Sex, Porn, and Fantasy Obsession in the Internet Age.* New York: Alyson Books, 2006.

BIBLIOGRAPHY

Arora, Raksha. "Are Americans Really Abject Workaholics?" Gallup
Poll Commentary, October 5, 2004, www.gallup.com/poll/13291/
Americans-Really-Abject-Workaholics.aspx.

Black, Claudia. *My Dad Loves Me, My Dad Has a Disease: A Child's
View Living with Addiction,* 3rd ed., San Francisco: Mac
Publishing, 1997.

Carnes, Patrick. *Out of the Shadows: Understanding Sexual Addiction,*
3rd ed. Center City, MN: Hazelden, 2001.

Crawford, Christina. *Mommie Dearest.* New York: William Morrow, 1978.

Fisher, Helen. *Why We Love: The Nature and Chemistry of Romantic
Love.* New York: Macmillan, 2005.

Good, G. E., Thoreson, P., and Shaughnessy, P. "Substance Use,
Confrontation of Impaired Colleagues, and Psychological
Functioning among Counseling Psychologists: A National Survey."
Counseling Psychologist 23(4), 703–21, 1995.

Hughes, P. H., Baldwin, D.C., Sheehan, D.V., et al.: "Resident
Physician Substance Use, by Specialty." *American Journal of
Psychiatry* 149, 1348–54, 1992.

Jones, Penny. *The Brown Bottle.* Center City, MN: Hazelden, 1983.

Miller, Alice. *The Drama of the Gifted Child: The Search for the True
Self.* New York: Basic Books, 2008.

Nace, E., Davis, C., and Hunter, J. "A Comparison of Male and Female
Physicians Treated for Substance Use and Psychiatric Disorders."
American Academy of Psychiatrists in Alcoholism and Addictions
4(2), 156–62, 1995.

O'Connor, P. G., and Spickard, A. "Physician Impairment by Substance Abuse," *Medical Clinics of North America* 81 (1997) 1037–52.

Robinson, Bryan. *Chained to the Desk: A Guidebook for Workaholics, Their Partners and Children, and the Clinicians Who Treat Them.* New York: NYU Press, 2001.

Willett, Edward, "The Chemistry of Love," online column, 2000, www.edwardwillett.com/Columns/lovechemistry.htm

Wills-Brandon, Carla. *Am I Hungry or Am I Hurting? Healing from Food Addiction with the Twelve Steps.* San Diego: RPI Publishing, 1993.

———. *Eat Like a Lady: A Guide to Recovery from Bulimia.* Deerfield Beach, FL: Health Communications, Inc., 1989.

———. *Is It Love or Is It Sex? Why Relationships Don't Work.* Deerfield Beach, FL: Health Communications, Inc., 1989; An Authors Guild Backinprint.com ed. Bloomington, IN: iUniverse, 2000.

———. *Learning to Say No: Establishing Healthy Boundaries.* Deerfield Beach, FL: Health Communications, Inc., 1990; An Authors Guild Backinprint.com ed. Bloomington, IN: iUniverse, 2000.

———. *Natural Mental Health: How to Take Control of Your Own Emotional Well-Being.* Carlsbad, CA: Hay House, 2000.

Woititz, Janet. *Marriage on the Rocks: Learning to Live with Yourself and an Alcoholic.* Deefield Beach, FL: Health Communications Inc., 1986.

———. *Self-Sabotage Syndrome: Adult Children in the Workplace.* Deerfield Beach, FL: Health Communications, Inc., 1989.

Young, Kimberly. *Tangled in the Web: Understanding Cybersex.* Bloomington, IN: First Books Library, 2001.

Carla Wills-Brandon is a licensed marriage and family therapist and a licensed psychological associate with a master's degree in clinical psychology. She is also the author of eleven books on topics including relationships, sexuality, addiction, self-esteem, trauma and recovery, spirituality and death and dying. She has appeared on numerous television programs and has lectured across the United States and the United Kingdom.

Carla graduated with honors from California State University at Fresno, with a degree in clinical psychology. She then went on to receive a master's clinical psychology from the California School of Professional Psychology at Fresno, an APA–approved institution. In her search for alternatives for patients suffering from food addictions, she also completed a two-year course of study and dissertation in a Doctor of Holistic Nutrition program at Clayton College of Natural Health.

She is married to Michael Brandon, PhD, a licensed child psychologist. Carla and Michael have been together since 1975 and have two sons, Aaron and Joshua. They live on Galveston Island in a hundred-year-old historic home with four cats, one dog, two birds, a turtle, and a tarantula. When they aren't on Galveston Island, Carla and Michael can be found in a small cabin in the Appalachian Mountains just outside of Asheville, North Carolina.

Contact Information
E-mail: BeyondtheChase@sbcglobal.net

Hazelden, a national nonprofit organization founded in 1949, helps people reclaim their lives from the disease of addiction. Built on decades of knowledge and experience, Hazelden offers a comprehensive approach to addiction that addresses the full range of patient, family, and professional needs, including treatment and continuing care for youth and adults, research, higher learning, public education and advocacy, and publishing.

A life of recovery is lived "one day at a time." Hazelden publications, both educational and inspirational, support and strengthen lifelong recovery. In 1954, Hazelden published Twenty-Four Hours a Day, the first daily meditation book for recovering alcoholics, and Hazelden continues to publish works to inspire and guide individuals in treatment and recovery, and their loved ones. Professionals who work to prevent and treat addiction also turn to Hazelden for evidence-based curricula, informational materials, and videos for use in schools, treatment programs, and correctional programs.

Through published works, Hazelden extends the reach of hope, encouragement, help, and support to individuals, families, and communities affected by addiction and related issues.

For questions about Hazelden publications, please call **800-328-9000** or visit us online at **hazelden.org/bookstore**.